The Bhagavad Gītā

Alexandre Piatigorsky is Professor of Religious Studies at London University teaching Indian philosophy and Buddhism. After lecturing in Moscow, he came to England in 1974. His publications include *A Buddhist Theory of Mind and Consciousness* and *Mythological Deliberations*.

Element Classics of World Spirituality

The writings and teachings of the great spiritual masters are brought together in the *Element Classics of World Spirituality* series. These volumes focus on the philosophical and religious meaning of the texts and their abiding relevance. They are introduced by internationally recognized scholars and spiritual leaders, who highlight and enhance the richness and depth of the writings.

In the same series

The Cloud of Unknowing
The Dhammapada
The Pilgrim's Progress
Rumi's Divan of Shems of Tabriz
The Tao Te Ching

ELEMENT CLASSICS OF
WORLD SPIRITUALITY

The Bhagavad Gītā

Introduced by Professor Alexandre Piatigorsky

Translated by J A B van Buitenen

ELEMENT
Rockport, Massachusetts • Shaftesbury, Dorset
Brisbane, Queensland

First published in 1997 by
Element Books Limited
Shaftesbury, Dorset

Published in the USA in 1997 by
Element, Inc.
42 Broadway, Rockport, MA 01966

Published in Australia in 1997 by
Element Books Limited
for Jacaranda Wiley Limited
33 Park Road, Milton, Brisbane 4064

Cover design by Bridgewater Book Company
Page design by Linda Reed
Typeset by Footnote Graphics, Warminster, Wilts.
Printed and bound in USA by Courier Westford Inc, Westford

British Library Cataloguing in Publication
data available

Library of Congress Cataloging in Publication
data available

ISBN 1-85230-917-2

The approach of J A B van Buitenen to this text does not necessarily accord with that of the present author. Professor van Buitenen's own views are expressed in his introduction to the full text in *The Bhagavadgita in the Mahabharata: Text and Translation*, which is available from the University of Chicago Press.

Contents

Introduction

The Philosophy of the Bhagavad Gītā

The *Bhagavad Gītā* is part of the sixth book of the great ancient Indian epic, the *Mahābhārata* (the longest book in the history of mankind). Although not very long – only some forty pages in English translation – the *Gītā* is extremely dense in meaning and thought. As the book itself claims, it is clearly meant to be understood, *in one way or another*, by all people, but in fact it can only be understood by very few because there are so many ways to interpret it and too many possible positions from which it may be tackled. It also should be emphasized that the *Gītā* itself quite explicitly allows for all these positions and variants for it was created as a *general and universal* instruction on how to understand one's Self, one's world and one's God, even though it was communicated to one particular person within one particular, almost 'historical', situation. This circumstance alone makes the *Gītā* a philosophical work.

Let us begin our tentative and preliminary understanding of the *Gītā* by looking at 'instruction' and its protagonists, ie, the instructor and the instructed. The story is a well-known one. On 18 February 3102 BC (the time is mythological, but does it matter?), on the eve of the great battle on the Field of Kuru (the place is real – about two hours by bus from New Delhi), the great warrior and chief of the Pāṇḍavas, Arjuna, requested his charioteer, friend and brother-in-law, Kṛṣṇa, to drive him to the centre of the battlefield so that he could see the two armies that were already drawn up against one another. When he saw on the opposing side his relations, old friends and teachers, Arjuna was filled with despair and said to Kṛṣṇa that he would rather be killed or become a miserable beggar than kill those with whom he was connected by ties of blood or friendship.

In reply, Kṛṣṇa explained to Arjuna that he, as well as everybody else, is Self (*ātman*), that there has been no time when he or they did not exist, and there will be no time when he or they will not exist, for Self cannot kill or be killed. Passing from one body to another, one's Self only changes its clothes or, as a bird, its nest, remaining always itself, unchanged and eternal. To this Kṛṣṇa added that while Arjuna and other people did not know their previous lives (when they had been reborn in different bodies) He, Kṛṣṇa, knew them all.

He also said that this battle on the Field of Kuru was not just a simple battle, one of many, but a great battle to mark the end of the previous (*dvāpara*) and the beginning of the next (*kāli*) period of time (*yuga*) – the period of history proper, so to speak. All other battles and wars to come would be no more than superfluous and senseless imitations of this one, which is witnessed (and by inference *designed*) by Him, the Highest Witness, Self of all Selves (*paramātman*), Person of all Persons (*puruṣottama*), the Highest God.

The great warrior, Arjuna, for whom the coming battle on the Kurukṣetra, however great, was still an ordinary battle, gained from Kṛṣṇa not only the knowledge that this battle was *Dharmic*, and the only *real* battle, but also *another* knowledge or, more precisely, a knowledge of this event as *another* event. The knowledge of what the battlefield and the battle are in reality is not an ordinary knowledge, for no reality can be seen by ordinary eyes or heard by ordinary ears. That is why Kṛṣṇa, the Lord, endows Arjuna, an ordinary man, with supernatural vision and hearing, and the battlefield becomes the final scene in the interplay between Divine Cosmic Forces, hitherto inaccessible not only to ordinary men but also to the great sages and gods. In other words, the battlefield becomes a setting for Divine Instruction in a new philosophy and religion.

Driving the chariot to the middle of the battlefield,

while an extra-ordinary act in a 'natural' sense – for only a great leader of men would have placed himself between the two armies for the final stand-off – has also another meaning, which Arjuna himself could not have known, but Kṛṣṇa did. In this second meaning, the centre is a 'neutral' position of the 'Absolute Witness or Observer of the Field' (Kṣetra), the Universe (or Micro-Universe, ie, the body). It is the place where 'everything may happen'. In Arjuna's case what occurs is a meeting with God (previously only vaguely or half-recognized), during which he partakes of an infinitesimal fragment of His Divine Knowledge – and the centre of the battlefield is the 'natural' place for this to happen.

The philosophy of the introductory episode of the *Gītā* contains, in fact, an answer to the often repeated question 'what is what?' – where the second 'what' is a thing or event (or an idea), and the first is that which only the *Knower* (here Kṛṣṇa the Lord) knows. Everything is not what it seems – or what we think it is – and there can be no philosophy at all without this precondition. Thus, let me repeat, Arjuna did not know the meaning of the battlefield of Kurukṣetra or of the battle itself. Nor did he know who Kṛṣṇa was, or who he himself was. Kṛṣṇa explains to Arjuna that the battlefield is the Field of *Dharma* and the battle is *dharmic*. He also explains that Arjuna is Soul, Self (*ātman*), and He, Kṛṣṇa, is God Absolute, simultaneously a human manifestation of himself in the form of Vāsudeva (son of Vāsudeva) and Devaki (Arjuna's friend, brother-in-law and charioteer) – and, more importantly, Arjuna's Self (Kṛṣṇa being the Self of all Selves) and his Instructor in Divine Knowledge.

Let us start with the first idea introduced in the *Bhagavad Gītā*, and ask, as did Arjuna (2:7), 'What is *dharma*?' *Dharma* (literally, 'that which holds', 'that which establishes') primarily denoted the order in which Vedic rituals were performed and the fulfilment of duties and rules incumbent on those who performed them. In the *Mahābhārata*, *dharma* became the all-embracing notion; the common denominator; the idea of the absolute, unchanging cosmic order. This cosmic order (the Law in van Buitenen's translation) reigns everywhere, and from top to bottom hierarchically. However, most importantly, as distinct from Roman, Greek, Jewish, Anglo-Saxon or European law (and also from 'natural law' or 'common justice'), *dharma* comprises not only *all that must be*, but also *all that there is to be, has to be*, and, in the final analysis, *all that there is, the way all things are. Dharma* is much broader than ethics or morals, for ethics and morals derive from *dharma*, not the other way round. In other words, not all that is good is *dharma*, but all that is *dharmic* is good by definition. When Arjuna complains to Kṛṣṇa that he does not want to kill his enemies because he feels it is *dharmically* wrong, Kṛṣṇa replies that to kill them is *dharmic* and therefore right – an explanation that the present-day reader may find hard to accept. If you are a warrior on the battlefield, your *dharma* is to kill your enemies, whether or not you wish to. Though later personified as a deity, *dharma* as a philosophical idea is impersonal – a framework of one's behaviour, be it the behaviour of the whole cosmos, a country, a class, a profession, or of an individual god, man or animal. Moreover, there are special *dharmas* for men and women, for the different periods in one's life, and for various family and personal relationships. All of these *dharmas* are, as it were, 'already established', and over all of them reigns the *dharma* of Kṛṣṇa the Lord. The latter, however, is an exception, for if everyone behaves and acts within his or her own *dharma*, Kṛṣṇa alone exercises His *dharma*, not being bound by it Himself. So it is from Kṛṣṇa that Arjuna learns that his unwillingness to kill his relations, though *dharmic* in terms of family *dharma*, is not *dharmic* in terms of the *dharma* of warriors, and this latter *dharma* is more important than the first, because the battle is about to begin in the place and at the time predetermined by Kṛṣṇa's universal *dharma*. Therefore, Arjuna must rise and fight, for his is the *dharma* of warriors. However, Arjuna does not want to kill his relations and friends, not only because he considers such killing unlawful (*adharma*) but because he does not *want* to do so, whether such an act is *dharmic* or not. Because Arjuna does not know what his *dharma* is, and which *dharma* is the more important, he does not know his own Self (*ātman*) – and this is the central idea of the *Bhagavad Gītā*. When Arjuna says that he does not want to kill his enemies, Kṛṣṇa explains that Self cannot kill or be killed, because it is eternal, unchanging, and indestructible. Moreover, and this is very important philosophically, when Arjuna received this knowledge it was as if he had never known it before, for each and every time the knowledge of *ātman* is communicated, it is *new*. And what is even more important, *ātman* itself is not an event, for it is not related to any other event in time and space; it figures in the *Gītā* as pure *being* and *knowing*. This means that, as such, it is not related to anything or anybody, which is not to say that nothing and nobody are related to it. On the contrary, it is through Kṛṣṇa's Divine Knowledge that Arjuna becomes related to Self by virtue of *his* knowledge of Self. But what, then, is Arjuna in this relation, and what is this relation? Arjuna is that which he knows, may know, or can know of (his own) Self: ie, to know that there is Self. (He cannot know Self, for it is Self that knows him, because it is not related to him.) This, however, is only one face of Arjuna, that facing *ātman* or himself as *ātman*. His other face is facing himself as a creature, a sentient being (*bhūta*, *sattva*) of one kind or other. (In both cases he is 'I' – 'I' as that which thinks of itself (or knows itself) as thinking on (or knowing) something that is not 'I'.)

Returning to what we have called 'event', we find in Arjuna a person (*puruṣa*, ie, that which is called and addressed as 'Arjuna'), an instructee, so to speak, in the knowledge of what he is and of what his 'instructor', Krishna the Lord, is – the knowledge of Self, *ātman*. It is that *ātman* which, when embodied ('possessor of body', *dehin*), can change its body as a man (*nara*) changes his clothes. However, what takes place (as an event) does not happen to or with *ātman*, nor to 'beings' in general (always referred to in the third person). It happens to only a named 'me' or 'thee' who is an actual or potential recipient of the 'higher' knowledge of *ātman*, or to someone who possesses the 'lower' knowledge about his bodies, about other beings and their bodies, and about the world. These two knowledges operate with the two respective 'organs' of knowledge, *buddhi* and *manas* (translated respectively as 'spirit' and 'mind' by van Buitenen). In other words, whatever happens (or whatever event we can speak, write or think of) happens in the space between one's 'I' and its *knowledge* of Self, and one's 'I' in its relation to the world of bodies and beings (including that very 'I' as a being and body). It is for such an 'I' that the term *puruṣa* was used in the *Gītā*, a term that approximates our idea of 'person'. Thus, in postulating Self, Kṛṣṇa at the same time postulates non Self, ie, the body with its five sensory organs, and mind as the sixth. From this it directly follows that all that one can kill, damage or affect in any way (including the 'I' which can be taught to understand this) is not Self but the body alone. This first and most fundamental *dualism* of the *embodied* (ie, Self) and his *body* opens the way to a whole series of philosophical dualisms, some of which are complementary, others are established within one of its two parts or introduced to characterize and concretize them. But all of these dualisms are introduced as Kṛiṣṇa's answers to Arjuna's explicit or implicit questions. One of the most interesting 'dualist' ideas (and at the same time the most alien to our habitual philosophical thinking – in fact it will be suspended and then cancelled in the course of our exposition) is that of Self versus Knowledge of Self. We read in the *Gītā* (5:21): 'The man who knows him [ie, Self] for what he is – indestructible, eternal, unborn, without end – how does he kill whom or have whom killed?' It follows from this passage that such knowledge of Self makes the knower as indestructible and eternal as (his) Self. This in turn means that the Knowledge of Self is Self, and that the Knower of Self (literally, 'a person who knows it') is Self too. This equation of epistemology (theory of knowledge) with ontology (theory of being, of Self), though it can be easily traced in the supposedly earlier texts, the *Upaniṣads*, is nowhere postulated with more clarity and precision than in the *Bhagavad Gītā*.

Another dualism postulated in the *Gītā* is that of 'that which really exists (*sat*), of what there is no un-becoming'/ 'that which does not really exist (*asat*), of what there is no becoming'. The underlying idea here is that Self (*ātman*) is uncreated and, therefore, has no part in cosmogony and, strictly speaking, is in no sense related to time. Self's *bodies* live in time in the beginningless continuum of his rebirths, whereas Self, 'unending embodied', is *immeasurable* (time = measure here) in the *creatures* he passes through. Only in them is he manifest and thinkable – as such he is *unmanifest* (*avyakta*), *unthinkable* (*acintya*) and *indestructible (akṣara)*. The complementary dualism of 'unmanifest/ manifest' is of special philosophical interest, because it establishes Self as *always* being in (or passing through) three phases: unmanifest, manifest, and unmanifest. 'Manifest' here means 'existing *in* creatures' (human, divine or animal), but is perceived, mistakenly, *as* a creature. 'Unmanifest' means existing outside the sphere and capacity of perception, for the last can only perceive the objects of the senses. Unmanifest is not only a disembodied Self but also a potentially embodied one: one that is waiting to become manifest as a concrete creature. In this latter sense, unmanifest implies a *philosophical uncertainty* with respect to the time or place (one of billions of universes or trillions of worlds) where a concrete creature can be found or detected. The infinite number of creatures through which a Self passes, manifest and unmanifest, implies the possibility that there can be no creature in the whole universe of universes through which a given Self would not have passed or will not pass at one time or another (remember that 'time' is used here only in relation to creatures, not to Self, which is timeless). This, in turn, gives rise to the idea of *one* Self for all creatures.

This leads on to the dualism of Self/Nature (*prakṛti*). Nature is that initial material (not matter!) of which all things animate and inanimate – together with the organs of sense, perception and mind that perceive them – are 'made'. However, the real basis of Nature is not the elements of earth, water, fire, air and ether which represent its static aspect, but the three dynamic forces (*guṇas*) of activity, passivity and their balance, which are constantly at work within one another and all of them together within each one, *ad infinitum*. It is due to these forces, or tendencies, that the whole phenomenal world exists, because working both in the objects and the organs of senses, they make possible not only sensation and perception but the whole of mental activity, including reasoning and intellect. To put it simply, we may say that Nature with its three forces is opposed to Self, as the dynamic and changing is opposed to the unchanging and eternal. At the higher level of knowledge, however, the dualism of Self/Nature is complemented by the dualism of the two natures of God: His lower Nature (ie, Nature with its three *guṇas*) and His higher Nature (comprising all creatures in their manifest and unmanifest states). The ultimate source of both Natures is Kṛṣṇa's own Divine Energy or *māyā*, Cosmic Delusion – delusion in the sense that ordinary people are deluded by it and are not able to discern Him behind His Divine Energy, or are unable to discern the immortal Self in a mortal creature. In this case, as in many others, in the philosophy of the *Bhagavad Gītā*, the dualism of the two Natures of Kṛṣṇa is superseded by the idea of his 'third' Nature, which is unknowable and mysterious, and outside all universes, all creatures and even all His own manifestations.

This exposition of philosophical dualisms could be extended further but, as every student of ancient Indian philosophy knows, an explanation of Knowledge (ie, 'what is what?' and 'what *art thou*?' in relation to this Knowledge) is impossible without postulating a special faculty or organ of higher cognition. So *buddhi* ('spirit' in van Buitenen's rendering) was introduced as *that by means of which* these universal dualisms are understood and become part of one's *higher mentality* (*mahat*, 'the great'). That Knowledge itself assumed the name of *Sāṃkhya* ('calculation', 'counting'), which is also the name of one of the most interesting schools of Indian philosophy. Sāṃkhya may be perceived as 'theory of dualisms' when the spirit is applied to the understanding of them. But the application of Spirit is also dual. After being applied to Sāṃkhya, it is applied to one's mental *discipline (yoga)*. Yoga (literally and etymologically 'yoke', 'yoking') is postulated in the *Gītā* as a *practice* by means of which a man can transform the Divine Knowledge revealed to him into himself, his body and mind. Then with his body and mind transformed *practically*, not only will he see the world and himself differently, but he will also become a totally different 'seer' of them. Yoga assumes here its philosophical meaning: like *dharma*, the universal denominator, yoga becomes the universal transformer. Thus everything becomes yoga – not only the consciously applied, special technical means, devices and methods that transform one's mind and behaviour, but also all the factors (physical and mental), events, facts and circumstances that change man and the universe. It is Kṛṣṇa the Lord who is the Master (or Sovereign) of Yoga (*Yogeśvara*), and who constantly changes, creates and recreates the Universe by His Divine Yogic Power (*māyā*).

This general meaning of yoga finds its concretization in the *philosophy of disinterested action* and the Yoga of Action (*karmayoga*). The philosophy of disinterested action is very simple. An ordinary, normal, (ie, *natural*) person's behaviour or action (*karman*) has three aspects: 1) the cause, motivation, or desire to act; 2) the act itself; 3) the result, or what he expects the result to be and which he sets as the purpose of the action. Such a threefold action binds its performer in two ways. First, the acting person, interested and involved (*sakta*) in his action, becomes bound by it psychologically and, being bound by action (*karma-bandha*), is totally unable to *know* either the action or himself as the acting person. Secondly, such a threefold action possesses objectively (ie, by virtue of its nature) the power which determines good or bad *karmic* effects in one's future rebirths, binding one to be reborn in good or bad conditions and, in the final analysis, determining whether one is reborn at all. In other words, it is the desire to act for the sake of the results of the action that brings about both the action and its far-reaching consequences (*karma*). Action without motivation, desire, need or expectation, without fear of failure or hope of success (ie, disinterested (*asakta*) action) is absolutely neutral and indifferent and therefore exempt from nature and its laws, as well as from the laws, rules and conventions of society. This action is, in fact, 'non-action', as distinct from normal, natural inaction motivated by laziness, passivity and the *desire not to act*. Moreover, this is the way in which Kṛṣṇa Himself is active, and the way which he asks Arjuna to follow when he urges him to fight.

But there is one other aspect of this concept. In the *Gītā*, the idea of action was taken from its priestly, *brahmanical* context, where action was conceived in the first place as a Vedic sacrifice, or one of its elements. With the *Gītā*'s idea of pure or disinterested action, a totally new standpoint was established, from which perspective only a sacrifice performed without any desire for reward would be considered real. From this it follows that any action whatsoever is, by definition, a sacrificial action, for such an action is a sacrifice to Kṛṣṇa, even if its performer does not know this. The last point is very tricky philosophically, because it again stresses the *objective* character of disinterested action – objective not only in the sense that such an action is devoid of any *subjective* motivation or intention, but also in the sense that it cannot, as such, be subjectively perceived by anyone other than Kṛṣṇa Himself. It remains purely internal, leaving no trace in the observable reality of ordinary life, and is witnessed only by the Self of its performer and by the eternal witness, the Self of all Selves, Kṛṣṇa.

The Yoga of Disinterested Action (*karmyoga*) combines the yogic ideas and practices current at the time of the creation of the *Gītā* with the innovative ideas and methods then in place and, more importantly, with a different kind of philosophical self-awareness of its own. Side by side with the classical yoga which found its completion in the *Yoga Sutras* of Patañjali – the two main methods of which are withdrawal of the senses from the objects of the senses, and all-absorbing mental concentration on a chosen yogic object ('single-mindedness' in the *Gītā*) – the Yoga of Disinterested Action offered the adept the idea of an *absolute neutralization* of the yogin's emotional, intentional and volitional acts and impulses. The Yoga of Knowledge, however, is the Knowledge of what is and what is not Self, of what is and what is not action, and of the *field* in which one's Knowledge directs and controls one's actions – because only the Knower knows that any action is a 'zero action' and that it is the field (ie, body, world, universe) which makes it a normal (natural, non-yogic) action. An adept may stop at this and remain a practitioner of the Yoga of Knowledge. But he can go further than this and begin to practise the Yoga of Action. Then he can be anything whatsoever – a soldier, a merchant, a carpenter, a blacksmith, a priest or a highway robber. This knowledge, translated into any sort of activity, makes him a *karma* yogin, a special kind of person who has already 'burnt all his actions', and acts only outwardly. In fact, and we see it everywhere in the *Bhagavad Gītā*, Knowledge is presented as the most essential factor underlying any yoga, because without the knowledge of what a yoga can transform into what, that yoga remains no more than one of many other specific activities – not the only all-transforming action, a universal 'anti-action', so to speak. On the other hand, Knowledge is that which informs the adept's behaviour and makes it a yoga, in the sense of 'the way' (*mārga*) leading to Kṛṣṇa. So we have the third yoga, the Yoga of Devotion (*bhaktiyoga*), in which the adept translates his Knowledge into his yogically transformed emotion of love for Kṛṣṇa. This threefold yoga reflects the natural division of men into three broad psychophysical types: intellectually active, active in action, and active in love. But it reflects also the three main modes of transformation of the 'natural' person into an 'inner' yogin, a perfect adept of Kṛṣṇa ('natural' in the sense that these modes correspond to the three *guṇas* of Nature (*prakṛti*).)

That universalized idea of 'yoga based on Knowledge' as an all-transforming activity – starting with Kṛṣṇa who transforms the universe and ending with the man who transforms his mind and body and thereby his world – has in the *Gītā* three very important *anthropological* consequences: 1) yoga becomes a universal analogue to, or substitute for, the *cult* in the *new religion* revealed to Arjuna by Kṛṣṇa; 2) the yogin is presented as a new *Universal Man* whose active participation in worldly activity is merely outward and nominal. All differences between human beings – ethnic, social, economic, linguistic, psychological, even religious – are thus also seen as outward and nominal, and therefore non-existent with respect to this yoga; 3) consequently, each and every human being is an actual or potential yogin of Kṛṣṇa.

So, what we have here is a concept of 'man–yogin' (*Homo Yogin*, so to speak) who – by knowing that everything which is not immortal Self does not exist, and that Kṛṣṇa the Lord is the eternal ground and axis for all things existing and non-existing – becomes, himself, immortal and eternal.

The most interesting thing about the concept of God in the *Gītā* is that Kṛṣṇa is not God in our sense of the word. Nor is Kṛṣṇa's philosophy of Self or Soul (*ātman*) and of Himself as the highest Self, a theology; it is, rather, a kind of religious philosophy. Each and every theology is, by definition, based on the initial postulate of an *absolute reality* of a personal God, from which follows the absolute reality not only of all forms in which God reveals Himself, but of all that is created by Him too.

Kṛṣṇa's person-ness is highly questionable, for in all His personal manifestations and descents – as a boar or wild man, as a fish or a prince – His *real* person, or Person of all Persons, remains not only separately existing, but totally transcendental, unknowable, and unthinkable. For, indeed, let us ask ourselves, can we conceive of Him as the whole universe, or as all-devouring Time and All-Absorbing Death? It would be enough to say that He manifests Himself *as* a person, friend, and in-law to Arjuna, and, further, as God. However, even God here is a metaphor, for in His teaching all gods are ousted to the realm of creatures, however highly placed, and to the realm of the natural – far inferior to the realm of his adepts, perfect yogins, knowers and devotees. But who is He in reality, or, more exactly, in *His* reality? For whatever is real to us would invariably remain non-real in relation to His ultimate being.

To this question, Kṛṣṇa answers with respect to creatures or sentient beings (ie, humans, gods, animals, etc): 'This village of creatures helplessly comes into being again and again and dissolves at the fall of night . . . only to be reborn at the Dawn of Day. But there is a being beyond that being [ie, beyond the being of all these creatures, when at Night, they abide in an Unmanifest state], an eternal Unmanifest beyond the Unmanifest, which, while all beings perish, does not itself perish . . . it is my supreme domain' (8:20–21). And further: 'All this world is strung on me in the form of the Unmanifest; all creatures exist in me, but I do not exist in them' (9:4–5). In that ultimate domain, there are no creatures, manifest or unmanifest, and no persons too, including Kṛṣṇa himself. Because when He says: 'The Unmanifest is my supreme domain', He says it *as* a person (Kṛṣṇa), but this domain is itself beyond any definition, human, divine, personal or impersonal. It can be referred to only philosophically, while having itself no reference to anything.

But what is the relation between God as the Highest Self (*paramātman*) and the individual Self? This is the most crucial question of all – for those unknown people who in ancient times heard (or read) the *Gītā*, as well as for the many generations who have come to it since. *Brahman* is introduced as that which can be regarded as the universal counterpart to the individual Self, but only *can be* – no straight opposition (*the universal/the individual*) is explicitly given. Moreover, these are only two of a series of six notions, explained in 8:3–4: 'The supreme *brahman* is imperishable. The individual self is called [one's] nature ... that brings about ... the being of the creatures is called act. The 'elemental' is transitory being; the spirit [ie, that which is not body made of the *elemental*] is the 'divine', and I myself am the 'sacrificial' here in this body.'

There are as many riddles as there are statements here. The imperishable supreme *brahman* is that which underlies the whole universe; it is its axis and sole fundament. Philosophically speaking, it is the most general, universal thing of all things thinkable and unthinkable, and the individual Self is the most individual thing of all. So, the opposition between them, as between the universal and the individual, seems to be clear and simple. But only *seems* to be, because the idea of individuality itself is very strange here. (The individual does not mean personal, for person in the *Gītā* is altogether different from self, *ātman.*) Moreover, simply to say this would be a mistake, for it would then be necessary to define the difference between them – which is impossible. But, finally, it would be possible to assert, in principle at least, that the individual Self, though it is of the nature of *brahman* (or its particular case), is opposed to *brahman* which is of its own nature (*svabhāva* – the term used to denote one's own nature in a natural sense). From this, however, it does not follow that they are the same. 'Act' here figures as the cause of the generation of creatures – the cosmic act of divine yogic power that, in the final analysis, supplies Self with its bodies. Thus, it can be said that it is his being as creature that makes the Self individual. 'The elemental' in this passage is the primary material of nature, of which the bodies (but not creatures) are created, in which the selves abide – and to which the divine spirit (*puruṣa*) is opposed. This last is a very abstract philosophical principle (belonging, in fact, to the philosophy of Sāṃkhya): it implies that nature and spirit are in this sense absolutely separated from one another. This different teaching, not dealing with creatures and individual selves, constitutes a separate line in the philosophy of the *Gītā*. But then we return to Kṛṣṇa who, as the 'sacrificial in the body' (ie, the object of all the sacrifices, thus identifying Himself with *brahman*), makes the universe homogeneous and imaginable as one, and as His universe.

It is here that Kṛṣṇa becomes the 'Supreme Person . . . the Sage and Preceptor primordial, more minute than an atom, creator of all, of form unimaginable' (8:8). The Supreme Person, however, is not a person, in either the metaphysical or ordinary sense of the word, for he is not God in these two senses. He is here the ultimate object of our thinking, which is, probably, the nearest possible approximation to our idea of God. This leads us to a very original definition of person – in any philosophy: 'A Person always becomes whatever being he thinks of when he at last relinquishes the body' (8:6). Thus, a person who dies thinking of Kṛṣṇa as Supreme Person, really becomes His person – a real adept of Him, a strange God, as it were, in the strange new philosophical religion of the *Gītā*.

We come now to the philosophy of time in the *Gītā*. Time is threefold. The first time is the 'quasi-historical' time of Kṛṣṇa's descents (*avatāra*) or, rather, time established by Him in his descents as a sequence of cycles (*yugas*), etc. (This is not *His* time, for He as the Self of all Selves (*paramātman*), is not *in* time). This time can be known by men (*nara*) and gods (*deva*) as the time of their lives, commensurable with their existences and experiences (knowledges), and *subjective* as far as it is experienced and known by them – though at the same time *objective*, since it was established by Kṛṣṇa *for* them. In fact, what we would call 'history' is this time, for history is always the time of something else – be it facts and events, Kṛṣṇa's descents, or the evolution of the entire organic and inorganic material world – and, therefore, different from and other than, time itself. All these 'objectivities' cannot be experienced or made experienceable *as* time, and can be thought of *in* time only on the strength of *another knowledge* issuing from a knower who places himself beyond the end of any event – in the way that Kṛṣṇa, while being manifested, remains outside all his manifestations in time and space.

The second kind of time in the *Gītā* is time during which a higher knowledge is communicated and perceived. Throughout the whole text this time is extraneous to knowledge itself, for the 'organ' of such a perception – mind (*manas*) – is extraneous to the Self of the perceiver. It is *natural*, for mind is an aspect of nature. On the one hand, it is presented by mind to itself as the *idea* of its own 'inner' *duration*, and on the other as its own fixation as one indivisible and separate *event* (an *event of knowledge*). This kind of time is very 'flexible' and exists only in relation to the knowledge one perceives and to one's (mental) capacity to perceive this knowledge. And indeed, when we learn from the text that Kṛṣṇa's entire conversation with Arjuna lasted only a couple of seconds (while the 'actual' time of its reading aloud would have amounted to no less than two and a half hours), we have to put this down to 1) the supernatural character of the message; 2) the transcendental character of the Knowledge; and 3) the supernatural character of the perception. This kind of time starts, continues and ends with the start, continuation and end of a described act (or event) of mind. From the point of view of a higher (let alone the highest) Knowledge of Kṛṣṇa, this time is nothing but a mere figment of human or divine imagination (corresponding to, respectively, the natural or supernatural mind, a *māyā* of a *māyā*). It is born and dies with an act of thought – not with the thinker, let alone the Divine One.

The third kind of time, postulated in the eleventh chapter of the *Gītā*, is not a cosmic trick or even the Cosmic Trickster; it is Kṛṣṇa (Viṣṇu) Himself as Time as Death – the supercosmic monster into whose gigantic gullet are sucked all *persons* existing from (or, more exactly, from before) the beginning of time (of both the first and second kinds), and 'the nearer they are to that monster's flaming mouth the more rapidly are they drawn in'. *What* persons? In general, *all* persons; in this particular case, almost all protagonists of the *Gītā*. All the extant persons in all the extant universes have been *designed and named* before the beginning of time and space; they are then thrown into the times and spaces of the various universes, through which they will travel until swallowed by Time as Death. From here they will emerge, reforged and remoulded, to be thereafter reshaped and renamed as other, different, persons.

Time here is not just a synonym of death. It means not only death in the sense of the end of one's flow of 'mental' time, but much more than that; Time in this passage is a *thing* or *entity*, not something in which other things or events happen in a temporal sequence. If anything, Time stays rather than moves, though in its *relative* movement it moves in the direction opposite to that of the 'normal' time of one's life or the course of events in history. Furthermore, as the factor that makes the conscious non-conscious, Time is opposed to 'normal' or 'mental' time (ie, the time of one's perception). It is described as the gigantic, black, 'anti-mind body' which swallows persons after having weakened their reason, churned their senses, and blunted their consciousness. The more non-conscious one becomes, the quicker one gravitates towards that massive Death-Time centre of the Mega-Universe of Viṣṇu.

> As moths on the wing ever faster will aim
> for a burning fire and perish in it,
> Just so do these men increasing their speed
> Make haste to your mouths to perish in them.
>
> You are greedily licking your lips to devour
> These worlds entire with your flickering mouths:
> Your dreadful flames are filling with fire,
> And burn to its ends this universe, Viṣṇu!

says Arjuna to Kṛṣṇa as the Mega-Universe (11:29–30).

But then a question arises: is Death itself – understood as 'anti-time' and opposite to the directional flow of 'normal' or 'mental' time – conscious of itself and of the Universe? Kṛṣṇa the Lord answers this question as follows:

> I am Time grown old to destroy the world,
> Embarked on the course of world annihilation:
> Except for yourself none of these [warriors] will
> survive,

. . . I myself have doomed them ages ago:
Be merely my hand in this, Left-handed Archer!
. . . Slay . . . my victims . . . destroy them and tarry not!

Here we see not 'Kṛṣṇa the Man', smiling, with radiant face and 'four-armed form', Arjuna's charioteer and very good friend, but the triad of Death, Time and Destiny. The crucial point in our understanding of the theme of Death is that, in terms of Time, Death can be reduced to two consciousnesses: the consciousness of Time at the end of time, as the final annihilation of the universe ('I am Time grown old . . .'), and the consciousness of that *dharmic design* (or Destiny) which preceded ('ages ago') the beginning of the 'normal' (or cyclic) time, when Viṣṇu 'had doomed them'. This brings us back to the conjecture that time is reduced to death or, more precisely, to that kind of consciousness which is styled 'death consciousness', and which is always ascribed to a *person.*

But what is a person in the *Gītā*? Unlike Self, who is timeless, and unlike a creature whose time is quasi-historical, a person is assigned by himself and his mind to a span of time that stretches from 'before the beginning' to his end. But a person does not know his own 'track' in time and space, only Kṛṣṇa, the Ancient Person, knows it, for He contains in His Being all spaces and times, His own included. In other words, Kṛṣṇa as the Highest Person is not only the 'author' of all the plots of all persons' lives, but also the protagonist and actor. In fact, again using a theatrical and literary metaphor, it is to the knowledge of one's life-plot that the idea of person can be reduced. A Self has no plot, but knows his 'field', ie, the sentient beings through which he passes; and a sentient being has no knowledge of itself for it has no organ of knowledge (*buddhi*). A 'person' is that which has a plot; and although he knows only his part and not the whole plot of his life, he possesses the latter knowledge potentially. This knowledge can be actualized, made known to him by *another*, God, Great Sage, etc. At the same time, a person is that which can communicate this knowledge to others, which a Self or a sentient being cannot do. There can be no 'organ of person-ness', for though initially conscious of himself and his life, all that a person can be conscious of (including his 'being conscious of') is determined *objectively* at his inception and death – in God's primary design and final remelting. ('A person is the bearer of destiny', S Weightman.)

This threefold scheme of time – quasi-historical time (or the time of Kṛṣṇa's manifestations), mental time, and Time as Death – is, I think, the fullest one can find in any ancient context, mythological, religious or philosophical. And the *Gītā*'s theory of Time is unique philosophically in its explanation of how a person is connected with and derived from time.

There is only one absolute reality in this philosophy – Selves or Souls (*ātman*); only one universal analogue of this reality, itself unmanifest but having an innumerable number of manifestations, one of which is Kṛṣṇa the Lord. But He, in His ultimate being, is the unmanifest beyond the unmanifest, unthinkable and indefinable, embracing infinite myriads of universes with their times and spaces, souls and persons, beings and creatures. And, finally, there is knowledge which makes one that which one knows, and makes all things postulated in the *Gītā* relative to one's individual knowledge. It is this idea of knowledge existing on so many different levels that makes the *Gītā* accessible to so many different people – and at the same time makes its understanding so difficult.

My hope in writing this introduction is that it will lead to a clearer understanding of the complex ideas contained within the *Bhagavad Gītā*, as they are set out in the text itself.

The Bhagavad Gītā

The Bhagavad Gītā

1

Dhrtarāṣṭra[1] *said:*

1 When in the Field of the Kurus, the Field of the Law,[2] my
troops and the Pāṇḍavas had massed belligerently, what
did they do, Saṃjaya?[3]

Saṃjaya said:

When King Duryodhana[4] saw the Pāṇḍava's army arrayed,
he approached the Teacher[5] and said, 'Look at that mighty
host of the sons of Pāṇḍu, marshalled by Drupada's
son,[6] your sagacious student! There are champions there,
great archers, the likes of Bhīma[7] and Arjuna in battle –
5 Yuyudhāna, Virāṭa, the great warrior Drupada,
Dhṛṣṭaketu, Cekitāna, the gallant king of the Kāśis, Purujit
Kuntibhoja, and the Śaibya, a bull among men, valiant
Yudhāmanyu and gallant Uttamaujas, Saubhadra[8] and the
Draupadeyas,[9] all good warriors. But now hear, best of
brahmins, about our outstanding men, the leaders of my
army, I mention them by name: yourself, Bhīṣma,[10]
Karṇa,[11] Kṛpa,[12] Samitiṃjaya, Aśvatthāman,[13] Vikarṇa, the
son of Somadatta, and many other heroes who are laying
down their lives for me, all experienced fighters with many
10 kinds of weapons. Their army, protected by Bhīma, is no
match for us, but this army, protected by Bhīṣma, is a
match for them. All of you, stationed at your positions,
must defend Bhīṣma at all passages!'

Then grandfather,[14] the majestic elder of the Kurus, roared loud his lion's roar, bringing joy to Duryodhana, and blew his conch. On a sudden, thereupon, conches, kettledrums, cymbals, drums and clarions were sounded, and there was a terrifying noise. The Mādhava[15] and

Pāṇḍava,[16] standing on their chariot yoked with the four
15 white horses, both blew their conches – Hṛṣīkeśa[17] his
Pāñcajanya. Dhanaṃjaya[18] his Devadatta. Wolf-belly[19] of
the terrible deeds blew his great conch Pauṇḍra, Nakula
and Sahadeva their Sughoṣa and Maṇipuṣpaka. The
Kāśi king, a great archer, the mighty warrior Śikhaṇḍin,[20]
Dhṛṣṭadyumna, Virāṭa and the undefeated Sātyaki,
Drupada[21] and all the Draupadeyas, O king of the earth,
and strong-armed Saubhadra, each blew his conch. The
sound rent the hearts of the Dhārtarāṣṭras[22] and reverber-
ated fearfully through sky and earth.

20 The ape-bannered Pāṇḍava,[23] seeing the Dhārtarāṣṭras
in position, lifted his bow when the clash of arms began, O
king, and said to Hṛṣīkeśa, 'Acyuta,[24] station my chariot in
between the two armies, far enough for me to see the eager
warriors in position – for, whom am I to fight in this
enterprise of war? I want to see the men who are about to
give battle, who have come together here to do a favour to
the evil-spirited Duryodhana.'

At Guḍākeśa's[25] words, O Bhārata, Hṛṣīkeśa stationed
25 the fine chariot between the two armies, before Bhīṣma,
Droṇa and all the kings, and he said to the Pārtha,[26] 'Behold
the Kurus assembled!' The Pārtha saw them stand there,
fathers, grandfathers, teachers, maternal uncles, brothers,
sons, grandsons, friends, fathers-in-law, and good com-
panions, in both armies. Watching all his relatives stand
arrayed, he was overcome with the greatest compassion,
and he said despairingly, 'Kṛṣṇa, when I see all my family
poised for war, my limbs falter and my mouth goes dry.
There is a tremor in my body and my hairs bristle. Gāṇḍīva
30 is slipping from my hand and my skin is burning, I am not
able to hold my ground and my mind seems to whirl. And
I see contrary portents, Keśava,[27] but I see no good to come
from killing my family in battle! I do not wish victory,
Keśava, nor kingship and pleasures. What use is kingship to
us, Govinda?[28] What use are comforts and life? The very

men for whose sake we want kingship, comforts, and joy,
stand in line to battle us, forfeiting their hard-to-relinquish
35 lives! Teachers, fathers, sons, grandfathers, maternal
uncles, fathers-in-law, grandsons, brothers-in-law, and
other relatives-in-law – I do not want to kill them, though
they be killers, Madhusūdana,[29] even for the sovereignty of
the three worlds,[30] let alone earth!

'What joy is left, Janārdana,[31] after we have killed the Dhārtarāṣṭras? Nothing but guilt will accrue to us if we kill these assassins![32] Therefore we must not kill the Dhārtarāṣṭras and our kin, for how can we be happy when we have killed family, Mādhava? Even if their minds are so sick with greed that they do not see the evil that is brought on by the destruction of family, and the crime that lurks in the betrayal of friendship, how can *we* fail to know enough to shrink from this crime, we who do see the evil brought on by the destruction of family, Janārdana?

40 'With the destruction of family the eternal family Laws are destroyed. When Law is destroyed, lawlessness[33] besets the entire family. From the prevalence of lawlessness the women of the family become corrupt, Kṛṣṇa; when the women are corrupt, there is class[34] miscegenation,[35] and miscegenation leads to hell for family killers and family. Their ancestors tumble, their rites of riceball and water disrupted.[36] These evils of family killers that bring about class miscegenation cause the sempiternal class Laws and family Laws to be cast aside. For men who have cast aside their family Laws a place in hell is assured, as we have been told.

45 'Woe! We have resolved to commit a great crime as we stand ready to kill family out of greed for kingship and pleasures! It were healthier for me if the Dhārtarāṣṭras, weapons in hand, were to kill me, unarmed and defenceless, on the battlefield!'

Having spoken thus, on that field of battle, Arjuna sat down in the chariot pit, letting go of arrows and bow, his heart anguished with grief.

2

Saṃjaya said:

1 Then, to this Arjuna who was so overcome with compassion, despairing, his troubled eyes filled with tears, Madhusūdana said –

The Lord said:

Why has this mood come over you at this bad time, Arjuna, this cowardice unseemly to the noble,[1] not leading to heaven, dishonourable? Do not act like a eunuch, Pārtha, it does not become you! Rid yourself of this vulgar weakness of heart, stand up, enemy-burner!

Arjuna said:

How can I fight back at Bhīṣma with my arrows in battle, or at Droṇa, Madhusūdana? Both deserve my homage, enemy-slayer!

5 It were better that without slaying my gurus
I went begging instead for alms in this land
Than that I by slaying my covetous gurus
Indulge in the joys that are dipped in their blood.

And we do not know what is better for us:
That we defeat them or they defeat us;
Dhṛtarāṣṭra's men are positioned before us,
After killing whom we have nothing to live for.

My nature[2] afflicted with the vice of despair,
My mind confused over what is the Law,
I ask, what is better? Pray tell me for sure,
Pray guide me, your student who asks for your help!

There is nothing I see that might dispel
This sorrow that desiccates my senses,
If on earth I were to obtain without rivals
A kingdom, nay even the reign of the Gods![3]

Saṃjaya said:

Having spoken thus to Hṛṣīkeśa, enemy-burner Guḍākeśa

10 said to Govinda, 'I will not fight!' and fell silent. And with a
hint of laughter Hṛṣīkeśa spoke to him who sat forlorn
between the two armies, O Bhārata –

The Lord said:

You sorrow over men you should not be sorry for, and yet
you speak to sage issues. The wise are not sorry for either
the living or the dead. Never was there a time when I did
not exist, or you, or these kings, nor shall any of us cease to
exist hereafter. Just as creatures with bodies[4] pass through
childhood, youth, and old age in their bodies, so there is a
passage to another body, and a wise man is not confused
about it. The contacts of the senses with their objects,
which produce sensations of cold and heat, comfort and
15 discomfort, come and go without saying, Kaunteya.
Endure them, Bhārata. The wise man whom they do not
trouble, for whom happiness and unhappiness are the
same, is fit for immortality.

There is no becoming of what did not already exist,
there is no unbecoming of what does exist:[5] those who see
the principles see the boundary between the two.[6] But
know that that on which all this world is strung is imperishable: no one can bring about the destruction of this
indestructible. What ends of this unending embodied,
indestructible, and immeasurable being is just its bodies –
therefore fight, Bhārata! He who thinks that this being is a
killer and he who imagines that it is killed do neither of
them know. It is not killed nor does it kill.

20 It is never born nor does it die:
Nor once that it is will it ever not be;
Unborn, unending, eternal, and ancient
It is not killed when the body is killed.

The man who knows him for what he is – indestructible,
eternal, unborn, without end – how does he kill whom or
have whom killed, Pārtha?

As a man discards his worn-out clothes
And puts on different ones that are new,
So the one in the body discards aged bodies
And joins with other ones that are new.

Swords do not cut him, fire does not burn him, water does
not wet him, wind does not parch him. He cannot be cut,
he cannot be burned, wetted, or parched, for he is eternal,
25 ubiquitous, stable, unmoving, and forever. He is the
unmanifest,[7] beyond thought, he is said to be beyond
transformation; therefore if you know him as such, you
have no cause for grief.

Or suppose you hold that he is constantly born and
constantly dead, you still have no cause to grieve over him,
strong-armed prince, for to the born death is assured, and
birth is assured to the dead; therefore there is no cause for
grief, if the matter is inevitable. Bhārata, with creatures
their beginnings are unclear, their middle periods are clear,
and their ends are unclear – why complain about it?

It is by a rare chance that a man does see him,
It's a rarity too if another proclaims him,
A rare chance that someone else will hear him,
And even if hearing him no one knows him,

30 This embodied being is in anyone's body forever beyond
killing, Bhārata; therefore you have no cause to sorrow over
any creatures. Look to your Law[8] and do not waver, for
there is nothing more salutary for a baron than a war that is
lawful.[9] It is an open door to heaven, happily happened
upon; and blessed are the warriors, Pārtha, who find a war
like that!

Or suppose you will not engage in this lawful war:
then you give up your Law and honour, and incur guilt.
Creatures will tell of your undying shame, and for one who
35 has been honoured dishonour is worse than death. The
warriors will think that you shrank from the battle out of
fear, and those who once esteemed you highly will hold you

of little account. Your ill-wishers will spread many unspeakable tales about you, condemning your skill – and what is more miserable than that?

Either you are killed and will then attain to heaven, or you triumph and will enjoy the earth. Therefore rise up, Kaunteya, resolved upon battle! Holding alike happiness and unhappiness, gain and loss, victory and defeat, yoke yourself to the battle, and so do not incur evil.

This is the spirit[10] according to theory;[11] now hear how
this spirit applies in practice,[12] yoked with which you
40 will cut away the bondage of the act.[13] In this there is no
forfeiture of effort, nor an obstacle to completion;[14] even
very little of *this* Law[15] saves from great peril. This one spirit
is defined here as singleness of purpose, scion of Kuru,[16]
whereas the spirits of those who are not purposeful are
countless and many-branched. This flowering language
which the unenlightened expound, they who delight in the
disputations on the Veda,[17] holding that there is nothing
more,[18] Pārtha, inspired by desires, set upon heaven – this
language that brings on rebirth as the result of acts and
abounds in a variety of rituals[19] aimed at the acquisition of
pleasures and power, robs those addicted to pleasures and
power of their minds; and on them this spirit, this single-
45 ness of purpose in concentration,[20] is not enjoined. The
domain of the Vedas is the world of the three *guṇas*:[21]
transcend that domain, Arjuna, beyond the pairs of opposites,[22] always abiding in purity, beyond acquisition and conservation, the master of yourself. As much use as there is in a well when water overflows on all sides, so much use is there in all Vedas for the enlightened brahmin.

Your entitlement[23] is only to the rite, not ever at all to its fruits. Be not motivated by the fruits of acts, but also do not purposely seek to avoid acting. Abandon self-interest, Dhanaṃjaya, and perform the acts while applying this singlemindedness. Remain equable in success and failure – this equableness[24] is called the application; for the act as

such is far inferior to the application of singleness of
purpose to it, Dhanaṃjaya. Seek shelter in this singlemind-
50 edness – pitiful are those who are motivated by fruits!
Armed with this singleness of purpose, a man relinquishes
here both good and evil *karman*.[25] Therefore yoke yourself
to this application – this application is the capacity to act.[26]
The enlightened who are armed with this singleness of
purpose rid themselves of the fruits that follow upon acts;
and, set free from the bondage of rebirth,[27] go on to a state
of bliss. When you have the desire to cross over this quag-
mire of delusion, then you will become disenchanted with
what is supposed to be revealed, and the revealed itself.[28]
When your spirit of purposiveness stands unshaken at
cross-purposes with the revealed truth, and immobile in
concentration, then you will have achieved the application.

Arjuna said:
What describes the man who stands in concentration, Keśava? What does the one whose insight[29] is firm say? How does he sit? How does he walk?

The Lord said:
55 A man is called one whose insight is firm when he forsakes
all the desirable objects that come to his mind, Pārtha, and
is sufficient unto himself. Not distressed in adversities,
without craving for pleasures, innocent of passion, fear and
anger, he is called a sage whose insight is firm. Firm stands
the insight of him who has no preference for anything,
whether he meets good or evil, and neither welcomes nor
hates either one. When he entirely withdraws his senses
from their objects[30] as a tortoise withdraws its limbs, his
insight stands firm. For an embodied man who does not
eat,[31] the sense objects fade away, except his taste[32] for
them; his taste, too, fades when he has seen the highest.

60 Even of a wise man who tries, Kaunteya, the whirling
senses carry off the mind by force. One should sit down,
controlling one's senses, *yoked*, and intent on me, for firm

stands the insight of him who has his senses under control.
When a man thinks about sense objects, an interest in them
develops. From this interest grows desire, from desire
anger; from anger rises delusion, from delusion loss of
memory, from loss of memory the death of the spirit,
and from the death of the spirit one perishes. When he
experiences the objects with senses that neither love nor
hate and are under his control, and thus has himself under
control, he attains to serenity. In a state of serenity all his
65 sufferings cease, for in one whose mind is serene, singleness
of purpose is soon fixed. The one who is not yoked has
no singleness of purpose; the one who is not yoked has no
power to bring things about; and he who does not bring
things about knows no serenity – and how can a man without serenity know happiness? For a mind that is amenable
to the ranging senses carries off a man's capacity for
insight, as the wind a ship at sea. Therefore the insight of
him is firm who keeps his senses entirely away from their
objects, strong-armed prince. The controlled man wakes in
what is night for all creatures, as it is night for the seer of
vision when the other creatures are awake.

70 If all objects of wishes flow into a man
As rivers flow into the ocean bed
Which, while being filled, stays unmoved to its depths,
He becomes serene, not the one who desires them.

The man who forsakes all objects of desire and goes about without cravings, possessiveness, and self-centredness becomes serene.

This is the stance on *brahman*, Pārtha: having achieved it one is not deluded. Maintaining this stance even in his last hour,[33] he attains to the *nirvāṇa* that is *brahman*.[22]

3

Arjuna said:

1 If you hold that insight is superior to action, Janārdana,

why then do you urge me on to fearful action? With quite contradictory words you seem to confuse my own insight. Therefore tell me definitively which is the course by which I will attain to the supreme good.

The Lord said:
I have of old propounded, prince sans blame, that in this
world there is a twofold position to take: for those who
uphold insight through a discipline of knowledge, for those
who uphold action through a discipline of action. A person
does not avoid incurring *karman* just by not performing
5 acts,[1] nor does he achieve success by giving up acts. For no
one lives even for a moment without doing *some* act, for the
three forces[2] of nature cause everyone to act, willy-nilly. He
who, while curbing the faculties of action,[3] yet in his mind
indulges his memories of sense objects is called a self-
deceiving hypocrite. But he who curbs his senses with his
mind, Arjuna, and then disinterestedly[4] undertakes the
discipline of action with his action faculties, stands out.
Carry out the fixed acts, for action is better than failure to
act: even the mere maintenance of your body does not
succeed without acting.

All the world is in bondage to the *karman* of action,
except for action for purposes of sacrifice;[5] therefore
engage in action for that purpose, disinterestedly,
10 Kaunteya. Prajāpati,[6] after creating creatures and sacrifice
together, said in the beginning: 'Ye shall multiply by it, it
shall be the cow that yields your desires. Give ye the Gods
being with it, and the Gods shall give ye being. And thus
giving each other being ye shall attain to the highest good.
Themselves enhanced in their being with sacrifice, the
Gods shall give ye the pleasures ye desire: he who enjoys
their gifts without return to them is but a thief.' The strict
who eat only what is left over after sacrificing are cleansed
of all taints, while the wicked who cook for themselves
alone eat filth.

Creatures exist by food, food grows from rain, rain
15 springs from sacrifice, sacrifice arises from action. This
ritual action, you must know, originates from the *brahman*
of the Veda,[7] and this *brahman* itself issues from the
Syllable *OṂ*.[8] Therefore the ubiquitous *brahman* is forever
based upon sacrifice. He who does not keep rolling the
wheel[9] that has been set in motion, indulging his senses in a
lifespan of evil, lives for nothing, Pārtha. On the other
hand, a man who delights in the self, is satiated with
the self, is completely contented with the self alone, has
nothing left to do. He has no reason at all to do anything or
not to do anything, nor does he have any incentive of
personal interest in any creature at all. Therefore pursue
the daily tasks disinterestedly, for, while performing his
acts without self-interest, a person obtains the highest
20 good. For it was by acting alone that Janaka[10] and others
achieved success, so you too must act while only looking to
what holds together the world. People do whatever the
superior man does: people follow what he sets up as the
standard.

I have no task at all to accomplish in these three worlds,
Pārtha. I have nothing to obtain that I do not have already.
Yet I move in action. If I were not to move in action, untir-
ingly, at all times, Pārtha, people all around would follow
my lead. These people would collapse if I did not act; I
25 would be the author of miscegenation; I would assassinate
these creatures. The wise, disinterested man should do his
acts in the same way as the ignorant do, but only to hold the
world together, Bhārata. One should not sow dissension in
the minds of the ignorant, who are interested in their
actions: the wise man should take kindly to all acts, but
himself do them in a disciplined fashion.

At any rate, actions are performed by the three forces of
nature, but, deluded by self-attribution, one thinks: 'I
did it!' But he who knows the principles that govern the
distribution of those forces and their actions knows that

the forces are operating on the forces, and he takes no interest in actions. Because they are confused about these forces of nature, people identify with the actions of these forces, and he who knows it all has no reason to upset the slow-witted who do not.

30 Leaving all actions to me, with your mind intent upon the universal self, be without personal aspirations or concern for possessions, and fight unconcernedly. They who always follow this view of mine, believing it without disputing it, are freed from their *karman*. But those who do dispute and fail to follow my view, deluded in all they know, they, to be sure, are witless and lost.

Even the man of knowledge behaves according to his nature – creatures follow their natures: who will stop them? Love and hatred lie waiting in the sense and its object: one should not fall into their power, for they ambush one.

35 It is more salutary to carry out your own Law poorly than another's Law well; it is better to die in your own Law than to prosper in another's.

Arjuna said:
What is it that drives a man to commit evil, Vārṣṇeya,[11] however reluctantly, as though propelled by force?

The Lord said:
It is desire, it is anger, which springs from the force of
rajas,[12] the great devourer, the great evil: know that that is
the enemy here. This world is clouded by it as fire by
smoke, as a mirror by dust, as an embryo by the caul. The
knowledge of the conscient is covered by this eternal enemy
40 desire, Kaunteya, as by an insatiable fire. The senses, the
mind, and the spirit are said to be its lair: by means of them
it clouds knowledge and leads into delusion the one within
the body. Therefore, bull of the Bharatas,[13] first control
your senses, then kill off that evil which destroys insight
and knowledge.

The senses, they say, are superior to their objects; the mind is higher than the senses; the spirit is higher than the mind; and beyond the spirit is he.[14] Thus knowing the one beyond the spirit, pull yourself together and kill desire, your indomitable enemy, strong-armed prince!

4

The Lord said:

1 I propounded this imperishable Yoga to Vivasvat.[1] Vivasvat
transmitted it to Manu;[2] Manu told it to Ikṣvāku.[3] Thus
came down the tradition of Yoga which the royal seers
knew. Over a long span of time this Yoga was lost on earth,
enemy-burner. What I have propounded to you today is
this same ancient Yoga, treating you in so doing as my loyal
follower and friend, for this is the ultimate mystery.

Arjuna said:

But your birth is recent: Vivasvat's birth belongs to the distant past! How am I to understand that you 'propounded it in the beginning'?

The Lord said:

5 I have known many past births, and so have you, Arjuna. I
remember them all, while you do not, enemy-burner.
Although indeed I am unborn and imperishable, although
I am the lord of the creatures, I do resort to nature, which
is mine, and take on birth by my own wizardry.[14] For
whenever the Law languishes, Bhārata, and lawlessness
flourishes, I create myself. I take on existence from eon to
eon, for the rescue of the good and the destruction of the
evil, in order to reestablish the Law. He who knows thus
the divinity, as in fact it is, of my birth and work, no more
10 returns to rebirth when he dies – he returns to me, Arjuna.
There have been many who, rid of passions, fears, and
angers, and made pure by the austerities of insight, have
immersed themselves in me, resorted to me, and become of
one being with me. I share in them in the manner in which

they turn to me; for in all their various ways men do follow my trail, Pārtha.

People offer up sacrifices to deities when they want their actions to be crowned with success; for in this world of men the success that follows action follows swiftly. I have created the society of the four classes with due regard for the various distribution of the *guṇas* and the range of their workings: know that I am its author, and that I am forever without *karman*. Actions do not stick to me, for I have no yearning for the fruits of my actions: he who understands
15 me in this way is himself no longer bound by his own actions. The ancient aspirants to release also performed their acts in this same spirit; therefore you too must perform the same act which the ancients performed long ago.

Even wise men are confused about what is 'action' and what is 'non-action' – let me tell you what 'action' is, and when you know it you shall be free of evil. For one should know about action, know about misaction, and know about non-action – the course of 'action' *is* complex. He is possessed of the right spirit who is able to discern that there is no *karman* in action,[5] while there is *karman* in non-action; if he among all men is yoked with this spirit he can perform any act. The wise call that man a sage all of whose undertakings are devoid of the intention to achieve an object of desire, for his *karman* has been burned off by the
20 fire of insight. If one engages in an act while forgetting about its fruit, being already fully satisfied and in need of nothing, one does not incur any *karman* at all. He is not polluted when he does only bodily acts, without any expectations, keeping mind and self[6] controlled, and renounces all possessions. Contented with anything that comes his way, beyond the pairs of opposites, without envy, and equable in success and failure, he is not bound, even though he acts.

All the *karman* of one who acts sacrifically[7] dissolves

when he is disinterested and freed, and has steadied his
thoughts with insight. *Brahman* is the offering, *brahman*
is the oblation that is poured into the *brahman* fire by
brahman:[8] he who thus contemplates the act as nothing but
25 *brahman* must reach *brahman*. There are yogins who
regard sacrifice as directed to deities; others offer up
sacrifice by sacrificing into the fire that is *brahman*. Others
offer the senses[9] of hearing and so forth into the fires of
restraint, while others sacrifice the objects of sound, etc,
into the fires of the senses. Others again offer up all the
actions of the senses and those of the vital faculties into
the wisdom-kindled fire of the yoga of self-restraint. There
are sacrificers who offer with substances, others with
austerities, others with yoga, others with knowledge and
Vedic study – ascetics all and strict in their vows. Some
sacrifice *prāṇa* into *apāna*[10] and *apāna* into *prāṇa*, blocking
the passage of *prāṇa* and *apāna* as they practise breath
30 control. Others limit their meals and offer *prāṇas* into
prāṇas. All of them know the meaning of sacrifice and
destroy their evil with sacrifice. Living on the elixir that
is the remnants of their sacrifice, they go to the eternal
brahman. This world is not of him who fails to sacrifice –
could then the higher world be his, best of Kurus?

Thus sacrifices of many kinds are strung in the mouth
of *brahman*;[11] know that they all spring from action, and
knowing this you shall be free. The sacrifice of knowledge is
higher than a sacrifice of substances, enemy-burner, but all
action culminates in knowledge, Pārtha. Know this: The
men of wisdom who see the truth shall teach you their
knowledge, if you submit to them, put questions to them
35 and attend to them. Armed with their knowledge you will
no more fall victim to confusion, and through it you
will see all creatures without exception within yourself and
then within me. Even if you are the worst criminal of them
all, you will cross over all villainy with just your lifeboat of
knowledge. Just as a blazing fire reduces its kindling to

ashes, Arjuna, so the fire of knowledge makes ashes of all
karman. For there is no means of purification the like of
knowledge; and in time one will find that knowledge within
oneself, when one is oneself perfected by yoga. The believer
40 who is directed to it and has mastered his senses obtains
the knowledge; and having obtained it he soon finds the
greatest peace. The ignorant and unbelieving man who is
riven with doubts perishes: for the doubter there is neither
this world nor the next; nor is there happiness.

Acts do not bind him who has renounced his *karman* through yoga, cut down his doubts with knowledge, and mastered himself, Dhanaṃjaya. Therefore cut away this doubt in your heart, which springs from ignorance, with the sword of knowledge: rise to this yoga and stand up, Bhārata!

5

Arjuna said:

1 You praise the relinquishment of acts and at the same time the practice of them, Kṛṣṇa. Now tell me decidedly which is the better of the two.

The Lord said:

Both the renunciation and the practice of acts lead to the supreme good; but of these two the practice of acts is higher than the renunciation of acts. He is to be counted a perpetual renouncer who neither hates nor desires, for, strong-armed prince, if one transcends the pairs of opposites, one is easily freed from bondage. Only fools propound that insight and the practice of acts are different things, not the wise: by undertaking one you find the full fruit of both.

5 The adepts of insight and the adepts of practice reach one and the same goal: he sees truly who sees that insight and practice are one and the same. True renunciation is hard to accomplish without the practice of yoga, but armed with yoga the sage soon attains to *brahman*. Armed with

yoga, pure of soul, master of self and senses, identifying
himself with the selves of all creatures, he is not tainted
even though he acts. The man of yoga, knowing the truth,
knows that while seeing, hearing, touching, smelling,
eating, walking, sleeping, breathing, speaking, eliminating,
grasping, opening and closing his eyes, he does in fact do
nothing, as he realizes that it is only the senses operating on
their objects.

10 If one places all *karman* on *brahman* and acts disinterestedly, he is no more stained by evil than a lotus petal by
muddy water. Yogins do their acts with body, mind, spirit,
and even the senses disengaged, in order to purify the self,
without any interest in the acts themselves. The man of
yoga, renouncing the fruits of his acts, reaches the peace
of the ultimate foundation, while the undisciplined man,
who acts on his desires because he is interested in fruits, is
fettered by *karman*. Having renounced all *karman* with the
mind, the soul dwells, happy and masterful, in its nine-
gated fortress,[1] neither doing nor causing acts.

The Lord has not created into people either authorship
of acts, or the acts themselves, or the concatenation of act
15 and fruit: that is the doing of Nature.[2] The lord does not
take on any act's evil or good *karman*; ignorance obscures
insight – that is why people get confused. Of those, however, who have destroyed this ignorance about the self with
true knowledge, this knowledge illumines like a sun that
supreme reality. Their spirits directed to it, their selves into
it, founded on it, devoted to it, they no more go to return
again,[3] for their knowledge has cleansed away the taints.

Wise are they who see no difference between a learned,
well-mannered brahmin, a cow, an elephant, a dog, and
an eater of dogs.[4] In this very world they have conquered
creation whose minds are rooted in disinterest. For
brahman is without flaws and indifferent, and therefore
they are rooted in *brahman*.

20 He should not rejoice upon finding pleasure, nor

sadden when meeting the unpleasant: the knower of
brahman who stands upon *brahman* is steady of spirit and
harbours no delusions. Disinterested in outer sense
impressions, he finds the happiness that is in himself; his
spirit yoked with the yoga of *brahman*, he tastes a happiness
that is permanent. Indeed, the pleasures that spring from
sense impressions are sources of unhappiness, because they
have beginnings and ends, Kaunteya, so the wise man does
not indulge in them. The man who in this very life, before
he is freed from his body, is able to withstand the driving
force that gathers from craving and anger, is yoked, is
happy. When he finds happiness within, joy within, light
within, this man of yoga becomes *brahman*, attains to the
25 beatitude that is *brahman*. This beatitude that is *brahman* is
achieved by the seers whose evil has been cast off, whose
doubts have been resolved, who have mastered themselves
and are dedicated to the wellbeing of all creatures. The
beatitude that is *brahman* lies before the ascetics who are
rid of craving and anger, who have tamed their thinking
and know themselves. Keeping outside the impressions
from the outside world, centring the gaze between the
eyebrows, evening out inhalation and exhalation within
the nostrils, controlling senses, mind, and spirit, totally
devoted to release, with no trace left of desire, fear, or
anger, the seer is released forever. Knowing that I am the
recipient of sacrifices and austerities, the great lord of all
the world, the friend of all creatures, he attains serenity.

6

The Lord said:

1 He who performs the task set for him without interest in its
fruit is the true renouncer and yogin, not the one who does
not maintain the fire and fails to perform the rites.[1] Know,
Pāṇḍava, that what they proclaim as 'renunciation' is
precisely this discipline, for no one becomes a man of
discipline without abandoning the intention of fruits.

When a sage wishes to rise to this discipline, action is called
his means; when he has risen to this discipline, serenity
is called his means. For he is said to have risen to the
discipline only when he is interested no longer in sense
objects, no longer in his acts, but has renounced all
5 intentions. Let him by himself save himself and not lower
himself, for oneself alone is one's friend, oneself alone
one's enemy. To him his self is a friend who by himself has
conquered himself; but when the man who has not
mastered himself is hostile, he acts as his own enemy. To
him who has mastered himself and has become serene,
the higher self is completely stable, in cold and heat, in
happiness and unhappiness, in honour or abuse. Contented in his insight and knowledge, firm on his peak,
master of his senses, looking with the same eyes on a lump
of clay, a rock, or a piece of gold, he is called a yogin who is
truly 'yoked'. He is set apart by his equanimity before
friends, allies, enemies, uninvolved parties, neutrals, hateful folk, and relatives, before good men and evil ones.

10 Let the yogin yoke himself at all times, while remaining
in retreat, solitary, in control of his thoughts, without
expectations and without encumbrances. Let him set up for
himself a firm stool in a pure spot, neither too high nor too
low, with a cover of cloth, deerskin, or *kuśa* grass. As he sits
on his seat, let him pinpoint his mind, so that the workings
of mind and senses are under control, and yoke himself to
yoga for the cleansing of his self. Holding body, head, and
neck straight and immobile, let him steadily gaze at the tip
of his nose, without looking anywhere else. Serene, fearless,
faithful to his vow of chastity, and restraining his thinking,
let him sit yoked, his thought on me, his intention focused
15 on me. When he thus yokes himself continuously, the
yogin of restrained thought attains to the peace that lies in
me, beyond *nirvāṇa*.[2]

Yoga is neither for him who eats too much or not at all,
nor for him who sleeps too much or keeps himself awake,

Arjuna. Sorrow-dispelling yoga is his who has curbed his
meals and diversions, curbed his motions in activities,
curbed his sleeping and waking. He is called 'yoked' when
his restrained mind has come to rest upon his self alone and
he is without craving for any object of desire. Just as a
candle flame outside a draught does not flicker – that is the
well-known metaphor of a yogin of restrained mind who
yokes himself to the yoga of the self.

20 When thought ceases, curbed by the practice of yoga,
when he himself looks upon himself and is contented with
himself, when he knows a total bliss beyond sensual pleasure, which can be grasped by the spirit alone, and when he
knows it and, once fixed upon it, does not truly stray from
it, when he has acquired it and can think of no greater
acquisition, when firm on it he cannot be swayed even by
profound grief – then he knows that this is the unbinding
of his bond with sorrow, which is called 'yoga', and that this
yoga must be yoked on him decisively with undespairing
heart.

Renouncing without exception all objects of desire that
are rooted in intentions, taming the village of his senses all
25 around with his mind, he should little by little *cease*, while
he holds his spirit with fortitude, merges his mind in the
self, and thinks of nothing at all. Wherever his volatile
mind might stray unsteadily, he halts it and subdues it in
the self. For a higher bliss engulfs the yogin whose mind is
at peace, whose passions are appeased – who has become
brahman, with no more taints.

Yoking himself always in this manner, the taintless
yogin effortlessly savours the infinite bliss that is the touch
of *brahman*. Yoked in yoga, he sees himself in all creatures,
all creatures in himself – he sees everything the same.

30 When he sees me in everything and sees everything in
me, I will not be lost to him and he will not be lost to me.
He who shares in me as living in all creatures and thus
becomes one with me, he is a yogin who, however he

moves, moves in me. He is deemed the ultimate yogin, Arjuna, who, by comparing everything with himself, sees the same in everything, whether it be blissful or wretched.

Arjuna said:
Madhusūdana, this yoga you propound as equanimity, I cannot see how it would stay stable, because we are changeful: for, Kṛṣṇa, the mind is always changing, whirling, domineering, and tough – I see it as no more susceptible to control than wind itself!

The Lord said:
35 No doubt at all, strong-armed prince, the mercurial mind is hard to hold down. Yet, Kaunteya, it *can* be held, with tenacity and dispassion. While I agree that this yoga is hard to achieve for one who is not master of himself, it can be achieved with the right means by a self-controlled man who makes the effort.

Arjuna said:
Still, Kṛṣṇa, a non-ascetic who, while having faith, allows his mind to stray from this yoga before he achieves the ultimate success of yoga – what becomes of him? Does he not, like a shredded cloud, fade away, a failure either way,[3] strong-armed lord, without foundation and astray on the path to *brahman*? Pray resolve this doubt of mine completely, Kṛṣṇa, for no one can resolve this doubt but you.

The Lord said:
40 No, Pārtha, neither here nor hereafter is he lost, for no one who does good can go wrong, my friend. He goes to the worlds which are gained by merit,[4] and when he has dwelled there for years without end, this 'failed yogin' is born high in the house of pure and prosperous folk, or in the family of wise yogins: indeed, such a birth is quite rare in this world. There he will recover the purposiveness of his

previous life, scion of Kuru, and strive once more to perfect
it. For a person is sustained, even involuntarily, by his
previous application: desirous of knowing the yoga he
45 proceeds beyond the *brahman* that is the Veda. Then this
vigorously striving yogin goes the ultimate journey,
cleansed of evil and perfected in numerous lives. The yogin
surpasses the ascetics, surpasses even the sages who know,
surpasses the workers who merely act. Therefore, Arjuna,
become a yogin. Him I deem the most accomplished man
of yoga among all yogins who shares in me in good faith,
with his inner self absorbed in me.

7

The Lord said:

1 Hear how you, fixing your mind on me and finding
shelter in me, shall know me entirely beyond doubt, while
practising this yoga, Pārtha. I shall propound to you fully
that insight and knowledge, after acquiring which nothing
more remains to be known in this world. Among
thousands of people there is perhaps one who strives
toward success, and even among those who have striven
successfully, perhaps only one really knows me.

My material nature is eightfold, comprising the order
5 of earth, water, fire, wind, ether, mind, spirit, and ego. This
is my lower nature, but know that I have another, higher
nature which comprises the order of souls: it is by the
latter that this world is sustained, strong-armed prince.
Realize that all creatures have their source therein: I am the
origin of this entire universe and its dissolution. There is
nothing at all that transcends me, Dhanaṃjaya: all this
is strung on me as strands of pearls are strung on a string.
In water I am the taste, Kaunteya, in sun and moon the
light, in all the Vedas the syllable *OṂ*, in ether the sound,[1]
in men their manhood. In earth I am its fragrance, in the
sun its fire, in all creatures their vitality, in the ascetics their
10 austerity. Know, Pārtha, that I am the eternal seed of all

beings, I am the thought of the thinkers, the splendour of the splendid. I am the strength of the strong, but strength without ambition and passion. In the beings I am that desire that does not run counter to the Law, bull of the Bharatas. Know that all conditions of being, whether influenced by *sattva*, *rajas*, and *tamas*, come from me; but I am not in them: they are in me.

This entire world is deluded by these three conditions of being which derive from the *guṇas*, and thus it fails to recognize me who am in all eternity beyond the *guṇas*. For this miraculous world of my illusion which consists in the
three *guṇas* is hard to escape: only those who resort to me
15 overcome this illusion. The evil, deluded, vile men who do
not resort to me lose their wits to this illusion, and they are reduced to the condition of demons.

Four kinds of good men seek my love, Arjuna: the suffering, the seekers for knowledge, the seekers for wealth, and the adepts, bull of the Bharatas. Among them stands out the adept, who is loyal to me exclusively and is always yoked, for I am unutterably dear to him, and he is dear to me. All four are people of stature, but the adept I count as myself, for through his discipline he comes to me as his incomparable destination. Only after many a birth does the
adept attain to me, knowing 'Vāsudeva[2] is everything', and
20 a man of such great spirit is rare to find. Robbed of all true
knowledge by this desire or that, the others resort to other deities, while observing this or that restraint but themselves remaining constrained only by their own natures. Yet, whatever may be the divine body that any loyal person seeks to worship with faith, it is I who make his faith in that body unshakeable. Armed with that faith he aspires to propitiate that deity and obtains from it his desires – desires for which I in fact provide. However, the rewards of those of little wit are ephemeral: God-worshipers go to the Gods, but my loyal followers go to me.

To the unenlightened I am some unseen entity that has

become manifest, for they are ignorant of my transcendent
25 being, which is eternal and incomparable. Since they are
clouded by the illusion of my yoga,[3] I am opaque to all, and
the muddled world does not recognize me as unborn
and immortal.

Arjuna, I know the creatures of past, present, and
future, but no one knows me. Confused by the conflicts
that spring from desire and hatred, all creatures in creation
are duped into total delusion, Bhārata, enemy-burner. But
when finally the evil *karman* of righteous men has faded
away,[4] and they are freed from the confusions of conflict,
they devote themselves to me, firm in their vows. They who
strive toward freedom from old age and death by resorting
to me, know that *brahman* which is universal as well as
30 specific to every person: they know the act entire. They who
know me as 'elemental', as 'divine', and as 'sacrificial', until
their final hour, know me truly, with their spirits yoked.

8

Arjuna said:

1 What is that *brahman*? What is the individual self? What is
act, Supreme Person? What is called 'elemental', and what
'divine'? Who in this body is the 'sacrificial' one, and how is
he so, Madhusūdana? And how are you to be known by the
disciplined in their final hour?

The Lord said:

The supreme *brahman* is the imperishable. The individual
self is called nature.[1] And the outpouring that brings about
the origination of the being of the creatures is called act.
The 'elemental' is transitory being; the spirit[2] is the 'divine',
and I myself am the 'sacrificial'[3] here in this body, O best of
5 the embodied. He who leaves his body and departs this life
while thinking of me alone in his final hour, rejoins my
being – of that there can be no doubt. A person always
becomes whatever being he thinks of when he at last relinquishes the body, Kaunteya, for one is given being from its

being.[4] Therefore think of me at all times and fight: with mind and spirit fixed on me you shall beyond a doubt come to me. While thinking of the divine Supreme Person with a mind that is yoked to a discipline of practice and does not stray away from him, he goes to him, Pārtha.

The Sage and Preceptor primordial,
More minute than an atom, creator of all,
Of form unimaginable, hued like the sun
At the back of the night – who thus thinks of him

10 In his final hour with unshaken mind,
Armed with his devotion and power of yoga,
With his breath ensconced between his eyebrows,
Attains to the Person Supreme and Divine.

The abode that the Veda-wise call the eternal,
And the aspirants enter with passions shed,
And in search of which they practise the *brahman*,
I shall now propound to you summarily.

Closing all the doors of the senses and blocking the mind in
the heart and holding within the head the breath of the
soul, one embarks upon the retention of yoga. He reaches
the highest goal who relinquishes the body and departs life
while uttering the one-syllabled *brahman* that is *OṂ* and
thinking of me. He who thinks of me continuously without
ever straying in thought to another, that ever-yoked yogin
15 finds me easy to reach, Pārtha. When the great-spirited
travellers to the ultimate perfection reach me, they do not
return to rebirth, that impermanent domain of misery. All
the worlds, as far as the World of Brahmā,[5] return
eternally,[6] but once I have been reached there is no
more rebirth.

They know of days and nights who know the Day of Brahmā that lasts thousands of eons, and the Night that ends after thousands of eons. At the dawning of the Day all manifestations emerge from the unmanifest; at the falling

of the Night they dissolve in that self-same unmanifest.
This village of creatures helplessly comes into being again
and again and dissolves at the fall of Night, Pārtha, only to
20 be reborn again at the dawn of Day. But there is a being
beyond that being, an eternal Unmanifest beyond the
unmanifest, which, while all beings perish, does not itself
perish.

This Unmanifest, also called Akṣara, they declare to be that ultimate goal upon reaching which souls no more return – it is my supreme domain. It is the Supreme Person, attainable only through exclusive devotion, Pārtha, in whom the creatures inhere, the one on whom all this is strung.

I shall set forth the times at which the yogins departing
life return or do not return. The scholars of *brahman*
who depart life by fire, by sunshine, by day, in the bright
fortnight, and during the six months after the winter
25 solstice go to *brahman*. The yogin who reaches the light of
the moon by smoke, by night, in the dark fortnight, and
during the six months after the summer solstice returns.[7]
These two are considered to be the two routes of the world:
the white and the black; by the former one does not return,
by the latter one does return. No yogin who knows these
two routes is confused about them, Pārtha; therefore be at
all times yoked to yoga, Arjuna.

What reward of merit has been assigned
To rituals, Vedas, austerities, gifts,
All that merits the yogin who knows transcends
To attain the supreme, primordial place.

9

The Lord said:

1 I shall proclaim to you, who do not demur, this most
mysterious insight accompanied by knowledge which will
set you free of evil. It is the royal wisdom, the royal mystery,
the ultimate purification, which is learned from immediate

evidence, conforms to the Law, is easy to accomplish, and permanent. Men who do not believe in this doctrine of Law, enemy-burner, fail to reach me and they return to the runaround of deaths.

All this world is strung on me in the form of the
Unmanifest; all creatures exist in me, but I do not exist in
them. And again, the creatures do not exist in me[1] – behold
5 my supernal yoga![2] While sustaining the creatures and
giving them being, my self does not exist in them. Just as
the vast wind which goes everywhere is yet always
contained within space, so, realize this, all creatures are
contained in me. All creatures return to my nature at the
end of the eon, Kaunteya, and at the beginning of the eon I
create them again. Resting on my own nature I create, again
and again, this entire aggregate of creatures involuntarily
by the force of my nature.[3]

No acts bind me, Dhanaṃjaya, for I remain disinter-
10 ested and detached from all acts. Nature gives birth to the
standing and moving creatures under my tutelage,
Kaunteya, and for that reason does the world revolve.

The deluded disregard me in my human form, being
ignorant of my higher nature as the great lord of the
creatures. Mindless and futile in their expectations, actions
and knowledge, they abandon themselves to the deluding
nature of Asuras[4] and Rākṣasas.[5] But men of great spirit
who accept my divine nature venerate me uniquely. Pārtha,
knowing that I am the eternal source of the creatures.
There are those who, always yoked to devotion, adore me
and glorify me, while exerting themselves with fortitude,
15 and pay homage to me. Others venerate me, while sacrificing to me with the sacrifice that is knowledge, as one, or
several, or many, in my universal manifestations. I am the
rite, I am the sacrifice, I am the libation to the ancestors,
I am the herb,[6] I am the formula,[7] I am the butter,[8] I am
the fire, I am the offering. I am the father of this world,
its mother, the Placer and Grandfather, the object of

knowledge, the strainer,[9] the syllable *OṂ*, the *ṛc*, *sáman*, and *yajus*;[10] goal, master, lord, witness, abode, refuge, friend, source and destruction and continuity, container, imperishable seed. I shine and withhold rain or pour it out, I am immortality and death, the existent and the nonexistent, Arjuna.

20 The purified Vedic drinkers of Soma
Seek me with oblations to win their heaven;
And on reaching the blessed domain of Indra[11]
Enjoy the celestial joys of the Gods.

But upon enjoying the vast world of heaven,
Their merit exhausted, they rejoin the mortals;
Thus following devoutly the Law of the Vedas
And craving desires they come and they go.

But to those who serve me while thinking only of me
and none other, who are always yoked, to them I bring
felicity. Even they who in good faith devote themselves to
other deities really offer up their sacrifices to me alone,
Kaunteya, be it without proper rite. For I am the recipient
of all sacrifices and their master, though they do not really
25 recognize me and therefore slip. To the Gods go they
who are avowed to the Gods, to the ancestors go they who
are avowed to the ancestors, to the ghouls[12] go they who are
avowed to the ghouls, to me go they who sacrifice to me.

If one disciplined soul proffers to me with love a leaf, a
flower, fruit, or water, I accept this offering of love from
him. Whatever you do, or eat, or offer, or give, or mortify,
Kaunteya, make it an offering to me, and I shall undo the
bonds of *karman*, the good and evil fruits. He whose spirit
is yoked to the yoga of renunciation shall come to me. I am
equable to all creatures, no one is hateful to me or dear –
but those who share me with love are in me and I am in
30 them. Even a hardened criminal who loves me and none

other is to be deemed a saint, for he has the right conviction; he soon becomes Law-minded and finds peace forever. Understand this, Kaunteya: no servitor of mine is lost. Even people of low origins, women, *vaiśyas*, nay *śūdras*,[13] go the highest course if they rely on me, Pārtha. So how much more readily holy brahmins and devoted royal seers! Reduced to this passing world of unhappiness, embrace me! May your thoughts be toward me, your love toward me, your sacrifice toward me, your homage toward me, and you shall come to me, having thus yoked yourself to me as your highest goal.

10

The Lord said:

1 Again, strong-armed prince, listen to my supreme word
which, for your benefit I shall pronounce to you who
love me. Neither the hosts of Gods nor the great seers
themselves know my origin, for I am the beginning of
Gods and great seers all. He who knows me as the unborn,
beginningless great lord of the world, he among mortals
is undeluded and freed from all evil taints.

Insight, knowledge, lack of delusion, forbearance,
veracity, self-control, serenity, happiness, unhappiness,
5 becoming and unbecoming, fear and fearlessness, nonviolence, equableness, contentment, austerity, liberality,
renown, and dishonour – all the creatures' various modes
of life spring from me alone. The ancient seven seers and
the four Manus[1] from whom the creatures in the world
have issued were born of my being from my mind. He who
truly knows this ubiquity[2] and yoga of mine is himself
yoked to unshakeable yoga, no doubt of that. The wise,
who are filled with being,[3] love me in the knowledge that I
am the source of everything and that everything comes
forth from me. With their thoughts on me, their very lives
devoted to me, enlightening one another and always
10 recounting my stories,[4] they are full of contentment and

delight. To those who, always yoked, love me joyfully I grant the singleness of mind by which they attain to me. Residing in their own very being I compassionately dispel the darkness of their ignorance with the shining lamp of knowledge.

Arjuna said:
The divine seer Nārada[5] and all the seers declare that you are the supreme *brahman*, the supreme abode, the supreme means of sanctification, the divine and eternal Person, the primordial God, unborn and ubiquitous. So declare Asita Devala and Vyāsa,[6] and you yourself tell me so, Keśava, I know that all this is true; indeed neither Gods nor Dānavas[7] know your true manifestation, O lord. You yourself know yourself, Supreme Person, you who give being to the creatures, lord of the creatures, God of Gods, master of the world! Pray tell me of all your divine ubiquities, by means of which you permeate these worlds. How may I know you, yogin, in my constant meditations? In what various modes of being may I meditate on you, my lord? Tell me again fully of your yoga and ubiquity, Janārdana, for I am not sated of listening to your Elixir!

The Lord said:
Well then, I shall recount to you my divine ubiquities, best of Kurus, the chief ones, for there is no end to my plentitude.

I am the self that dwells in all beings, Guḍākeśa, I am the beginning, the middle, and the end of the beings. Of the Ādityas[8] I am Viṣṇu, of the celestial lights the shining sun, of the Maruts[9] I am Marīci, to the constellations I am the moon. Of the Vedas, I am the Sāmaveda, of the Gods I am Vāsava,[10] of the senses the mind, of the creatures the consciousness.[11] Of the Rudras[12] I am Śaṃkara,[13] the God of Riches am I to Yakṣas[14] and Rākṣasas, of the Vasus[15] I am the fire, of the mountains the Meru.[16] Know that of the priests I am their chief Bṛhaspati,[17] Pārtha, of marshals Skanda,[18] of the waters I am the ocean. Of the great seers I

am Bhṛgu,[19] of words the One Syllable,[20] of sacrifices the
prayer, of standing creatures the Himālaya.

Among all trees I am the Aśvattha,[21] of the divine seers
Nārada, of the Gandharvas[22] Citraratha, of the Siddhas[23] the
hermit Kapila. Know that among horses I am Uccaiḥśravas
born from the Elixir,[24] Airāvata[25] among grand elephants,
the king among his people. Of weapons I am the thunder-
bolt, of cows the Cow of Plenty,[26] I am Kandarpa[27] in
procreation, I am Vāsuki[28] of the snakes. I am Ananta[29]
among the Serpents, Varuṇa[30] among sea creatures,
30 Aryaman[31] among the Fathers, Yama[32] among those
who tame. Of the Daityas[33] I am Prahlāda, Kāla[34] among
things that count,[35] the lion among wild animals, Garuḍa[36]
among birds.

Of the means of purification I am the wind, among
armsmen Rāma,[37] among sea monsters the crocodile,
among rivers the Ganges. I am the beginning, middle, and
end of the creations, Arjuna, the wisdom of the self among
all wisdom, the debate of the disputers. I am the *a*
among syllables,[38] the *dvaṃdva*[39] among compounds, I am
everlasting Time, the Placer who looks everywhere, I
am all-snatching Death, and the Source of things yet to
35 be. Of feminines I am Fame, Beauty, Speech, Recollection,
Wisdom, Fortitude, and Patience. Of the Sāmans[40] I am the
Bṛhat, of meters the Gāyatrī,[41] of months Mārgaśīrṣa,[42] of
seasons Spring. Of gamblers I am the dicing game, of the
splendid the splendour; I am the victory, the resolution, the
courage of the courageous.

Among the Vṛṣṇis I am Vāsudeva,[43] among the
Pāṇḍavas Arjuna,[44] of the hermits I am Vyāsa,[45] of sages
Kavi Uśanas.[46] I am the stick of those who chastise, the
statesmanship of those who seek to triumph, the taciturnity
of the mysteries, the wisdom of the wise.

I am whatever is the seed of all creatures, Arjuna. Not a
40 being, standing or moving, can exist without me. There is
no limit to my divine ubiquities, enemy-burner: the full

extent of my ubiquity I have here merely indicated. Whatever beings have transcending power, lustre and might, know that each and every one of them has its source in a particle of my splendour. But what is the point to you of knowing this much, Arjuna? I support this entire universe with but a single portion of mine!

11

Arjuna said:

1 This ultimate mystery bearing upon the soul, which you
have propounded to me as a favour, has dispelled my delusion. I have heard from you in all detail the becoming and
unbecoming of the creatures, lotus-eyed one, and your
own indestructible greatness. Now I wish to set eye on
your real, supernal form, just as you have described
yourself, sovereign lord, Supreme Person! If you think that
I shall be able to look upon it, lord, master of Yoga, display
to me your imperishable person.

The Lord said:

Pārtha, behold my hundreds and thousands of shapes, of
many kinds, divine, in manifold colours and figures.
5 Behold the Ādityas, Vasus, Rudras, Aśvins,[1] Maruts;
behold, Bhārata, many marvels that have never been witnessed before. Behold the entire universe with standing and
moving creatures centred here in this body of mine –
and whatever else you desire to see. But you shall not be
able to look upon me with just your ordinary eyes: I shall
give you divine sight: behold my sovereign Yoga!

Saṃjaya said:

Having thus spoken, Hari,[2] the great sovereign of Yoga,
10 revealed to the Pārtha his supreme supernal form, with
countless mouths and eyes, displaying multitudes of
marvels, wearing numbers of divine ornaments, and raising
divine weapons beyond count. And this form wore celestial
garlands and robes, it was anointed with the perfumes

of the Gods – it was God himself, infinite and universal, containing all miracles.

If in the sky the light of a thousand suns were to rise at once, it would be the likeness of the light of that great-spirited One. In that body of the God of Gods the Pāṇḍava saw the entire universe centred, in its infinite differentiations. Dhanaṃjaya was stunned, and he shivered. He folded his hands, bowed his head and said –

Arjuna said:

15 I see all Gods in your body, O God,
And all creatures in all their varieties –
On his lotus seat the sovereign Brahmā,
The seers all and the snakes divine.

Your own infinitude stretching away,
Many arms, eyes, bellies, and mouths do I see,
No end do I see, no beginning, no middle,
In you, universal in power and form.

With diadem, mace, and discus endowed,
A mass of light ablaze on all sides,
I see you, so rare to behold, all around
Immeasurably burning like sun or the fire.

You are *Akṣara*, highest of truths to be known,[3]
The highest foundation of all this world,
Undying protector of Law sempiternal,
The Person Eternal I hold you to be.

Beginningless, middleless, endless, almighty,
Many-armed, with eyes that are sun and moon,
I see you with mouths that are blazing fires
Setting fire to this world with your incandescence.

20 All space that extends between heaven and earth,
All horizons are filled by you alone;
Having seen your dreadful and wondrous form
The three worlds shudder, great-spirited One!

For yonder the hosts of the Gods go into you –
Some laud you in fear with folded hands,
The throngs of the seers and Siddhas say Hail!
And sing your praise in long litanies.

Ādityas and Rudras, Vasus and Sādhyas,[4]
The All-Gods,[5] Asvins, Maruts and Fathers,
Gandharvas and Asuras, Yakṣas and Siddhas
Behold you amazed in all their numbers.

At the sight of your mass with its eyes and mouths,
Multitudinous arms, thighs, bellies, and feet,
Strong-armed One, and maws that are spiky with tusks
The worlds are in panic and so am I!

At the aspect of you who are brushing the sky,
Ablaze, many-hued, maws gaping, and eyes
Asparkle and wide, my innards are quaking,
And, Viṣṇu, I find neither firmness nor peace.

25 Just watching your mouths that bristle with fangs
And resemble the fire at the end of the eon,
I know no directions and find no shelter –
Have mercy, great God, repose of the world!

And yonder all sons of Dhṛtarāṣṭra
Along with the hosts of the kings of the earth,
Like Bhiṣma, Droṇa, that son of a *sūta*,[6]
Along with our own chief warriors too

Are hastening into your numerous mouths
That are spiky with tusks and horrifying –
There are some who are dangling between your teeth.
Their heads already crushed to bits.

As many a river in spate ever faster
Streams oceanward in a headlong rush.
So yonder heroic rulers of earth
Are streaming into your flame-licked mouths.

As moths on the wing ever faster will aim
For a burning fire and perish in it,
Just so do these men increasing their speed
Make haste to your mouths to perish in them.

30 You are greedily licking your lips to devour
These worlds entire with your flickering mouths:
Your dreadful flames are filling with fire,
And burn to its ends this universe, Viṣṇu!

Reveal to me, who are you so dread?
Obeisance to you, have mercy, good God!
I seek to encompass you who are primeval,
For I comprehend not the course you are taking.

The Lord said:
I am Time grown old to destroy the world,
Embarked on the course of world annihilation:
Except for yourself none of these will survive,
Of these warriors arrayed in opposite armies.

Therefore raise yourself now and reap rich fame,
Rule the plentiful realm by defeating your foes!
I myself have doomed them ages ago:
Be merely my hand in this, Left-handed Archer![7]

Slay Droṇa and Bhīṣma and Jayadratha,[8]
And Karṇa as well as other fine warriors –
My victims – destroy them and tarry not!
Wage war! You shall trounce your rivals in battle!

Saṃjaya said:
35 Upon hearing these words from Keśava
The Diademed Arjuna folded his hands,
And trembling he bowed and responded to Kṛṣṇa
In a stammer, prostrate, and terror-struck –

Arjuna said:

It is meet, Hṛṣīkeśa, that, hearing you praised,
The world is enraptured and flooded with love:
The terrified Rākṣasas flee to all regions,
The throngs of the Siddhas proffer their homage.

And why should they fail to bow down, great-souled One
Creator more worthy of honour than Brahmā?
Unending Lord God, repose of the world,
You're what is and is not and what is beyond it.

The Original God, the Person Eternal,
You are of this world the ultimate support,
The knower, the known, the final abode –
All is strung upon you, of infinite form:

Moon, wind, fire, Varuṇa, Yama are you,
Prajāpati are you, the great-grandfather,
I praise thee, I praise thee a thousandfold,
Once more and again I praise thee, I praise thee,

40 I praise thee in front, I praise thee in back,
I praise thee on every side, O All!
Of infinite vigour, of measureless might,
You encompass it all and therefore are all.

If, thinking you friend, I have to boldly
Cried, 'Yādava![9] Kṛṣṇa! Come here, my good friend!'
Not knowing of this your magnificence,
Out of absence of mind or sheer affection,

If perchance I have slighted you – merely in jest –
In matters of sport, bed, seating, or meal,
In privacy, Acyuta, or before others –
I ask your indulgence, immeasurable One!

Of the quick and the firm you are the begetter,
By all to be honoured the worthiest guru;
No one is your equal, still less then your better,
For in all three worlds your might has no bounds.

Therefore I bow low, prostrating my body,
And ask your forgiveness, worshipful Lord!
Pray bear with me, God, as a father with son,
As a friend with friend, as a lover with loved one.

45 At the sight of this unwitnessed marvel I thrill
While a sense of dread unsettles my mind:
Please show me, O God, the body I've known,
Have mercy, Lord God, repose of the world!

I wish now to see you again as before,
With your diadem, mace, and discus in hand,
Assume once again your four-armed form,
O thousand-armed One, embodied in all!

The Lord said:

Out of grace for you, Arjuna, have I revealed
By my power of Yoga my highest form,
Full of fire, universal, primeval, unending,
Which no one but you has ever beheld.

Not with Veda or rites, not with study or gifts,
Not with sacrifice or with awesome *tapas*[10]
Can I in this world be beheld in this form
By any but you, great hero of Kuru.

Have no more fear, be no longer bemused
By the sight of this form of me so awe-inspiring;
Your terror gone, your heart again pleased,
Set eyes once more on the body you know!

Saṃjaya said:

50 Quoth Vāsudeva to Arjuna
And showed him once more his form of before,
And put that terrified man to rest
By becoming again his gentle old self.

Arjuna said:

Now that I see your gentle human shape, Janārdana, I have come to my senses and my normal tenor is restored!

The Lord said:
You have seen this rarely revealed form that is mine: even
the Gods always yearn for a glimpse of this form. Thus, as I
am and as you have seen me, I cannot be seen with the aid
of the Vedas, austerities, gifts, and sacrifices. Only through
exclusive *bhakti*[11] can I be seen thus, Arjuna, and known as
55 I really am, and entered into, enemy-tamer. Only he comes
to me, Pāṇḍava, who acts for me, who holds me as the
highest, who is devoted to me without self-interest and
without any animosity against any creature.

12

Arjuna said:
1 Who are the foremost adepts of yoga: those who attend on
you with the devotion they constantly practise, or those
who seek out the imperishable that is unmanifest?[1]

The Lord said:
Those I deem the most adept at yoga who fix their minds
on me and in constant yoga and with complete faith attend
on me. But those who attend on the inexpressible unmanifest Imperishable, omnipresent, inconceivable, standing on
the peak,[2] immovable, and fixed, while they master their
senses and remain equably disposed to everyone and everything and have the wellbeing of all creatures at heart, those
5 reach me too. But it requires greater toil for those whose
minds are directed to the Unmanifest, for their goal is not
manifest and the embodied attain it with hardship. On the
other hand, those who, absorbed in me, resign all their acts
to me and contemplatively attend on me with exclusive
yoga, soon find in me their saviour from the ocean that
is the run-around of deaths, Pārtha, for their minds are
conducted to enter into me.

Fix your mind on me alone, let your spirit enter into me, and ever after you shall dwell within myself, no doubt of that. Or if at first you cannot hold your spirit firmly fixed on me, still cherish the desire to reach me by repeated yoga,

10 Dhanaṃjaya. Even if you are incapable of this repeated
application, be intent on acting for me, for by doing acts for
my sake you will also attain success. Or even if you are incapable of acting thus, though you are inclined to me, at least
restrain yourself and renounce the fruit of all your actions.
Knowledge is higher than study, contemplation transcends
knowledge, the relinquishment of the fruits of acts
surpasses contemplation, and upon resignation follows
serenity.

Without hatred of any creature, friendly and compas-
sionate without possessiveness and self-pride, equable in
happiness and unhappiness, forbearing, contented, always
yoked, mastering himself, resolute in decisions, with his
mind and spirit dedicated to me – such a devotee of mine is
15 beloved of me. Beloved of me is he who does not vex
the world and is not vexed by it, and who is free from
joy, intolerance, fear, and vexation. Beloved of me is the
devotee who is dependent on nothing, pure, capable,
disinterested, unworried, and who renounces all undertakings. Beloved of me is the devotee who neither hates nor
rejoices, does not mourn or hanker, and relinquishes both
good and evil.

A man who remains the same toward friend or foe,
in honour or dishonour, in heat or cold, in happiness and
misery, devoid of all self-interest, equable when praised or
blamed, taciturn, contented with anything whatever,
homeless, firm of mind, and devoted – such a man is dear
20 to me. Beloved above all are they who, faithful and
absorbed in me, attend to this elixir of Law I have set forth
to you.

13

The Lord said:

1 This body, Kaunteya, is called 'the field', and the ones who
know this call the one who knows this 'field' the 'guide' to
this field. Know, Bhārata, that I too am such a guide, but

to all the fields; this knowledge of guide and field I deem
knowledge indeed. Hear from me in summary what this
field is, what defines it, how it evolves and whence, and
who the guide is and what power he has. The seers have
chanted about them severally in various meters as well as
in definite statements corroborated by arguments in the
Brahmasūtras.[1]

5 The Elements,[2] the *ahaṃkāra,*[3] the *buddhi*, the Unmanifest, the ten Faculties,[4] the five Realms of these faculties,[5]
attraction, aversion, pleasure and displeasure, the bodily
organism, consciousness and continuity: this enumeration
is quoted in brief as constituting the field and its evolutes.[6]
Lack of pride, lack of display, lack of injury, forbearance,
uprightness, respect for one's teacher, purity, fortitude,
self-mastery, dispassion toward sense objects, lack of
self-pride, awareness of the faults inherent in birth, death,
old age, sickness, and unhappiness, lack of attachments,
lack of involvement with sons, wife, home, etc, constant
equanimity whether pleasing or displeasing events befall,
10 unstraying devotion to me through exclusive yoga, seeking
out a secluded spot, ungregariousness, constancy of
knowledge concerning the self, and insight into the import
of knowledge of real things – all this is declared to be
knowledge, and ignorance is its opposite.

I shall set forth to you that object of knowledge by
knowing which one attains to the beginningless *brahman*,
which is called neither existent nor nonexistent. Its hands
and feet stretching everywhere, its head and face looking in
every direction, its ears reaching out every way, it covers all
in the universe. While devoid of all the senses, it appears
to have the qualities of all of them; while disinterested, it
15 sustains all; while beyond the *guṇas*, it experiences the
guṇas. While within and outside the creatures, it is both
that which moves and that which stands; it is hard to know
because of its subtleness; and it is both far away and nearby.
Although undistributed, it appears distributed among the

creatures. It should be conceived of as at once sustaining,
bringing forth, and devouring the creatures. It is called
the light of lights beyond the darkness, the knowledge, the
object of knowledge and the goal of knowledge that abides
in the heart of everyone. Thus in short has been expounded
the field, and the knowledge that is to be had of it: my
devotee who achieves this knowledge is fit to share in
my being.

Know that Prakṛti and Puruṣa[7] are both beginningless,
20 and that Prakṛti is the source of the evolutes and the *guṇas*.
Prakṛti is stated to be a cause inasmuch as it is the agency in
the production of products, while Puruṣa is stated to be a
cause in that he experiences happiness and unhappiness.
For Puruṣa residing within Prakṛti experiences the *guṇas*
that spring from Prakṛti: his involvement with the *guṇas* is
the cause of births in either high wombs or low ones. The
Great Lord, also called Supreme Soul, is that transcendent
Puruṣa who is spectator, consenter, sustainer, and experi-
encer. He who thus knows Puruṣa, Prakṛti, and *guṇas* is not
born again, in whatever way he now exists.

There are those who by themselves see that soul in
themselves by means of introspection.[8] Others do so by
25 means of the yoga of acquired insight. Still others by means
of the yoga of action. And then there are those who, albeit
ignorant, hear of it from others and believe in it:
they too, true believers in what they hear, do overcome
death.

Whatever creature is born, whether moving or standing, springs from the union of 'field' and 'guide' – realize
that, bull of the Bharatas. He who sees the Supreme Lord
equally present in all creatures, not perishing while these
creatures perish, he sees indeed. When he sees the lord
equally present everywhere, he himself no longer hurts the
self and then goes the supreme journey. He who sees that
all actions are performed by Prakṛti alone and that the self
30 does not act at all, sees indeed. When he perceives that the

variety of beings have one centre from which all expand, then he is at one with *brahman*.

This imperishable self is transcendent because of its beginninglessness and its being beyond the *guṇas*. Although present in the body, Kaunteya, it does not act nor is it affected. Just as all-pervading space is not affected because it is too subtle, so this self, while present in every body, is not affected. Even as the one sun illumines the entire world, thus the owner of the field illumines the entire field, Bhārata. Those who with the eye of insight realize the boundary of field and guide, and the mode of separation from the Prakṛti of beings, attain the ultimate.

14

The Lord said:

1 Again I shall instruct you in the highest import of all
knowledge, the knowledge through which all hermits have
acquired supreme success. By absorbing this knowledge
they have reached my order of being and at periodic
creation are not reborn,[1] nor do they suffer at the time of
dissolution.[2]
The Large Brahman is womb to me: in it I plant the
seed, and thence the origination of all beings takes effect,
Bhārata. The Large Brahman is the original womb from
which the forms that are born from any wombs ultimately
issue, Kauteya, while I am the father who bestows the fruit.
5 The *guṇas* called *sattva*, *rajas*, and *tamas* are born from
Prakṛti, and they fetter the eternal embodied souls to their
bodies, strong-armed one. Among these *guṇas*, *sattva*,
which because of its spotlessness is illumining and salubri-
ous, binds the soul by means of an attachment to joy and
an attachment to knowledge, prince sans blame. Know
that *rajas* is characterized by passion and arises from
an attachment to craving; it binds the embodied soul by an
attachment to action, Kaunteya. Know, on the other hand,

that *tamas* arises from ignorance and deludes the embodied
souls; it binds through absentmindedness, sloth, and sleep,
Bhārata. *Sattva* attaches one to joy, *rajas* to activity,
Bhārata; *tamas* attaches one to negligence by obfuscating
knowledge.

10 *Sattva* predominates by suppressing *rajas* and *tamas*,
Bhārata; *rajas* by suppressing *sattva* and *tamas*, *tamas* by
suppressing *sattva* and *rajas*. When in all the faculties in the
body the light of knowledge shines forth, then one knows
that *sattva* is in full strength. When *rajas* predominates,
there arise greed, vigorous activity, enterprise, restlessness,
and passion, bull among Bharatas. Obscurity, indolence,
neglect, and delusion arise when *tamas* prevails, joy of the
Kurus. If the embodied soul dies when *sattva* reigns, he
attains to the pure worlds[3] of those who have the highest
15 knowledge. The one dying in *rajas* is reborn among people
who are given to acting; while one expiring in *tamas* is born
among the witless.

They say that the pure reward of correct action has the
nature of *sattva*, that the fruit of *rajas* is unhappiness, and
of *tamas* ignorance. From *sattva* rises knowledge, from
rajas greed, from *tamas* negligence, delusion, and ignorance. Those abiding in *sattva* go upward, those in *rajas*
stay in the middle, those who abide in the function of
tamas, the lowest of the *guṇas*, go downward.

When a man of insight perceives that no one but the
guṇas acts and knows the one who transcends the *guṇas*, he
20 ascends to my being. By transcending these three *guṇas*,
which are the sources of the body, the embodied soul rids
himself of the miseries of birth, death, and old age and
becomes immortal.

Arjuna said:
My lord, what are the signs by which one who transcends the *guṇas* may be known? How does he behave? And how does he overcome these three *guṇas*?

The Lord said:

That man does not abhor illumination, activism, and delusion when they are at work in himself, nor aspires to them
when they are not at work. A man is declared to have
transcended the *guṇas* when he sits aside as a disinterested
party, is not moved by the *guṇas* and does not react to
them, knowing that it is just the *guṇas* at work; who is
equable in happiness and unhappiness, self-contained,
equal-minded toward a lump of clay, a rock of gold, the
same toward the pleasing and the displeasing, imper-
25 turbable, facing blame and praise with equanimity, equable
in honour and dishonour, and toward friend and foe, and
who relinquishes all undertakings. He who attends on me
unstrayingly with the discipline of the yoga of devotion and
thus transcends the *guṇas* is fit to become *brahman*. For I
am the foundation of *brahman*, of the immortal and
intransient, of the sempiternal Law, and of perfect bliss.

15

The Lord said:

1 They speak of the eternal Aśvattha[1] tree whose roots are above, whose branches below, and whose leaves are the hymns: he who understands it understands the Veda.

> Its branches are stretching downward and up;
> They thrive on the *guṇas* with buds that are objects;
> The roots reach gradually down to the ground
> In the world of men, connecting with *karman*.
>
> No form can here be perceived of it,
> Neither end nor beginning nor final foundation –
> Cut down this Aśvattha so thoroughly rooted
> With the hardened axe of disinterest.
>
> Then try to seek out that singular spot
> Whence one does not return once he has found it:
> 'I draw near to that primordial Person
> From whom has derived this ancient impulse.'

5 Without pride or delusion or flaws of attachment,
Immersed in the self, all cravings abated,
From dualities freed, from joy and grief,
They attain, undeluded, that permanent spot.

Neither sun nor moon nor fire illuminate it, that supreme domain of mine, on reaching which they do not return. A particle of myself, as the eternal individual soul in the order of souls, pulls on the senses and mind that are part of Prakṛti, the master who takes on a body and again escapes it, transmigrating out of it with these senses as the wind moves on with the scents it has taken from their sources. He is the one who oversees the workings of hearing, sight, touch, taste, smell, and thought and thus savours the
10 objects. Whether he departs from or remains in the body, or experiences things according to the *guṇas* – the deluded do not perceive him: only those with the eyesight of knowledge do. The yogins who exert themselves see him reside within themselves, but those who have not mastered themselves and lack insight do not see him, however hard they try.

Know that it is my light that in the sun illumines the entire universe, the light that is in moon and sun. Permeating the earth I support the creatures with my power; I nurture all the herbs as the Soma endowed with all tastes. As the digestive fire lying within the bodies of living beings, I consume with the aid of *prāṇa* and *apāna*[2] the four kinds of food.[3]

15 I dwell in the heart of everyone,
From me spring memory, knowledge, and reason;
I am known through the knowledge of all the Vedas,
I make the Vedānta,[4] I know the Veda.

In this world there are two Persons, the transient and the intransient. The transient comprises all creatures, the intransient is called the One-on-the-Peak. There is yet a third Person, whom they call the Supreme Soul, the

everlasting lord who permeates and sustains the three
worlds. Inasmuch as I have passed beyond the transient
and transcend the intransient, therefore I am, in world and
in Veda, renowned as the Supreme Person.

He who is rid of his delusions and knows me thus as
the Supreme Person knows all there is to know; and he
20 partakes of me with all his being, Bhārata. Thus have I
declared to you, prince sans blame, this most mysterious
doctrine: by understanding it one becomes an awakened
man who has completed his task, Bhārata.

16

The Lord said:

1 Fearlessness, inner purity, fortitude in the yoking of
knowledge, liberality, self-control, sacrifice, Vedic study,
austerity, uprightness, noninjuriousness, truthfulness, peace-
ableness, relinquishment, serenity, loyalty, compassion for
creatures, lack of greed, gentleness, modesty, reliability,
vigour, patience, fortitude, purity, friendliness, and lack of
too much pride comprise the divine complement of virtues
of him who is born to it, Bhārata. Deceit, pride, too much
self-esteem, irascibility, harshness, and ignorance are of
5 him who is born to the demonic complement, Pārtha. The
divine complement leads to release, the demonic to
bondage. Have no qualms, Pāṇḍava, you have been born
to the divine. There are two kinds of creation in this world,
the divine and the demonic. I have spoken of the divine in
detail, now hear from me about the demonic, Pārtha.

Demonic people do not know when to initiate action
and when to desist from it; theirs is neither purity, nor
deportment, nor truthfulness. They maintain that this
world has no true reality, or foundation, or God, and is not
produced by the interdependence of causes. By what then?
By mere desire. Embracing this view, these lost souls of
small enlightenment are with their dreadful actions capable
10 of destroying this world they seek to hurt. Embracing this

'desire', which is insatiable, they go about, filled with the intoxication of vanity and self-pride, accepting false doctrines in their folly and following polluting life rules. Subject to worries without measure that end only with their death, they are totally immersed in the indulgence of desires, convinced that that is all there is. Strangled with hundreds of nooses of expectation, giving in to desire and anger, they seek to accumulate wealth by wrongful means in order to indulge their desire. 'This I got today, that craving I still have to satisfy. This much I have as of now, but I'll get more riches. I have already killed that enemy,
others I still have to kill. I am a master, I enjoy, I am
15 successful, strong and happy. I am a rich man of high
family; who can equal me? I shall sacrifice, I shall make donations, I shall enjoy myself', so they think in the folly of their ignorance. Confused by too many concerns, covered by a net of delusions, addicted to the pleasures of desire, they fall into foul hell. Puffed up by their egos, arrogant, drunk with wealth and pride, they offer up sacrifices in name only, without proper injunction, out of sheer vanity.

Embracing egotism, overbearing strength, pride, desire, and anger, they hate and berate me in their own bodies and
in those of others. Those hateful, cruel, vile, and polluted
20 men I hurl ceaselessly into demonic wombs. Reduced to
demonic wombs birth after birth, and deluded, they fail to reach me, Kaunteya, and go the lowest road. The gateway to hell that dooms the soul is threefold: desire, anger, greed – so rid yourself of these three. The man who is freed from these three gates to darkness, Kaunteya, and practises what is best for himself, goes the highest road. He who throws away the precepts of teachings and lives to indulge his desires does not attain to success, nor to happiness or the ultimate goal. Let therefore the teaching be your yardstick in establishing what is your task and what is not, and, with the knowledge of what the dictates of the teaching prescribe, pray do your acts in this world.

17

Arjuna said:

1 People who sacrifice outside the injunctions of the
teaching, yet are full of faith, what foundation do they
have, Kṛṣṇa, that of *sattva*, of *rajas*, or of *tamas*?

The Lord said:

In embodied souls Faith is of three kinds: according to a
person's nature it is typed as *sattva*, *rajas*, or *tamas*. Listen.
Everyone's faith conforms to this nature, Bhārata: a person
is as good as his faith. He is what his faith makes him.
Creatures of *sattva* sacrifice to Gods; creatures of *rajas* to
Yakṣas and Rākṣasas; creatures of *tamas* to ghosts and
5 ghouls. Men who practise awful austerities not provided
for by the texts, and practise them out of exhibitionism and
egotism, as they are filled with desires and passions,
mindlessly wracking the composite of elements in their
bodies, and me to boot within their bodies, know that
their own persuasion is demonic.

The preferred food of everyone is also of three kinds, as
are their sacrifices, austerities, and donations; hear the
specifics. Those kinds of food which increase lifespan,
mettle, vigour, health, comfort, and pleasure, and are tasty,
bland, fortifying, and agreeable are preferred by *sattva*
creatures. *Rajas* creatures like foods that are bitter, sour,
salty, very hot, sharp, rough, and burning, and that cause
10 discomfort, misery, and sickness. The *tamas* person prefers
food that is stale, has lost all taste, smells badly, is kept
overnight, even polluted leftovers.

Sattva rules a person who offers up sacrifices found in
the injunctions which are performed by those who do not
covet their fruits, and observes them in the pure conviction
that the sacrifice must go on. Of the *rajas* type, best of
Bharatas, is the sacrifice that is offered up both to obtain
the fruit and to display oneself. They call a sacrifice ruled by
tamas when it is not enjoined, lacks nourishing ingredients,

is unaccompanied by Vedic *mantras*, carries no priestly
stipend, and requires no faith.

Askesis of the body comprises homage to Gods, brahmins, gurus, and sages; purity; uprightness; continence;
15 and nonviolence. Askesis of speech comprises speech that
does not hurt, is veracious, pleasant, and beneficial, as well
as the recitation of the daily lesson. Askesis of the mind
comprises serenity of mind, gentleness, taciturnity, self-
control, and inner purity. This triple askesis practised with
the highest faith by committed men who expect no rewards
is of the nature of *sattva*. Askesis that is practised with
ostentation and in order to gain the reputation and homage
attendant on pious deeds is said to be of the *rajas* type,
and is ephemeral and unstable. Askesis undertaken under
foolish misconceptions, by means of self-molestation, or to
effect another's downfall is of the *tamas* type.

20 That donation is known to be of the nature of *sattva*
which is bestowed upon one who has not been a benefac-
tor, in the simple conviction that gifts must be given, at the
right time, in the right place, to the right recipients. A
donation is of the *rajas* type when it is made defectively,
with the purpose of repaying another or with a view to a
later reward. A donation is characterized by *tamas* when it
is made at the wrong place and time and to unworthy
recipients, without proper hospitality and in a contemptu-
ous manner.

OṂ tat sat[1] is the traditional triple designation of *brahman*; with it were of yore ordained the brahmins, the
Vedas, and the sacrifices. Therefore among those who
profess *brahman*, the acts of sacrifice, donation, and askesis
as prescribed by the injunctions always proceed after
25 invoking *OṂ*. The acts of sacrifice, and askesis, and those
of donation in all their variety, are performed by those who
wish for release and covet no mundane reward, while
pronouncing *tad*. *Sat* is used for that which is and that
which is good. Thus the word *sat* is used for any laudable

act, Pārtha. *Sat* is also used for sacrifice, donation, and askesis; any act involving these is styled *sat*. But the sacrifice offered up, the donation bestowed, and the askesis practised without faith is called *asat*, Pārtha; and it has no existence, either here or hereafter.

18

Arjuna said:

1 Strong-armed Hṛṣīkeśa, I wish to hear the nature of relinquishment and renunciation, and what sets them apart,
Slayer of Keśin.[1]

The Lord said:

The wise call it 'relinquishment' when one gives up
acts that are motivated only by desires, while they call
'renunciation' the renouncing of all fruits of acts. Some
teachers propound that all acting should be renounced, as
it is all tainted; while others hold that such acts as sacrifice,
donation, and askesis are not to be renounced.

So hear from me, best of the Bharatas, tiger among men,
the decision about what is renunciation. Of renunciation
5 there are declared to be three kinds. Acts of sacrifice,
donation, and askesis are *not* to be renounced: They are
one's task – sacrifice, donation, and askesis sanctify the
wise. It is my final judgment, pārtha, that these acts are to
be performed, but with the performer renouncing all self-
interest in them and all their rewards. It does not do to
give up an act that is prescribed; giving acts up out of folly
is the inspiration of *tamas*. If one renounces an act out of
fear of physical hardship, because it is 'too difficult', his
renunciation is inspired by *rajas*. But renunciation is
regarded as inspired by *sattva* if one performs a prescribed
act because it is one's task, while renouncing all self-
interest in it and all reward from it. The wise renouncer
10 inspired by *sattva*, who has resolved his doubts, does not
hate an act because it is unpleasant, or like one because it is
pleasant. After all, no one who has a body can renounce all

acts completely: he is the true renouncer who renounces the fruits of his acts.

Now, there are three kinds of fruits to an act: disagreeable, agreeable, and mixed; but such is the *karman* of the nonrenouncers hereafter, but never of the renouncers. Hear from me, strong-armed prince, the five factors which in Sāṃkhyan doctrine are stated to lead to the successful performance of all acts: the realm of the object; the agent; the different means; the various sorts of action; and finally divine fate.[2] These five factors are present whatever act a man undertakes, whether with body, speech, or mind, and whether right or wrong. This being the case, when a man because of insufficient understanding looks upon himself as the sole agent, he is in error and does not see. He whose disposition is not dominated by his ego and whose understanding is not obscured, does not kill and is not bound by his act were he to kill off these three worlds.

There is a triple impulse to action: knowledge, its object, and its subject; while the act itself comprises these three: means, object, and agent. Knowledge, action, and agent are of three kinds, according to the prevailing *guṇa*. Hear then how this division has been set forth in the enumeration of *guṇas*. Know that that knowledge is of a *sattva* nature through which one perceives a single eternal being in all creatures, a being which, though parcelled out, is indivisible. The knowledge that divisively perceives just various forms as being distributed over all the creatures is of the nature of *rajas*. To *tamas* is assigned that knowledge which, though limited and devoid of substance, groundlessly fixes on one object as though it were all.

Action is of the nature of *sattva* when it is done as prescribed, without self-interest, without love or hate, by one who does not wish to reap the reward. Action is assigned to *rajas* when it is painfully done by one who wants to gain something or who is motivated by egotism. Of *tamas* is declared to be that action which is mindlessly

undertaken without considering consequences, possible
death or injury, and one's own capacity for it.

An agent is of the nature of *sattva* when he is free from
self-interest, self-effacing, filled with fortitude and enterprise, and undisturbed by success and failure. He is of *rajas*
when he is passionate, covetous of the fruits of his actions,
greedy, injurious, impure, and filled with joy and grief. He
is assigned to *tamas* when he is undisciplined, instinctive,
insolent, crooked, deceitful, lazy, defeatist, and procrasti-
nating.

Likewise hear the triple divisions, determined by
guṇa, of intelligence and fortitude, as they are described
30 severally and in sum, Dhanaṃjaya. That intelligence
proceeds from *sattva*, Pārtha, which understands when to
act and when not, what is a task and what not, what is a
cause of fear and what not, what is bondage and what
deliverance. To *rajas* goes the intelligence with which one
incorrectly perceives Law and lawlessness, task and non-
task. An intelligence is inspired by *tamas*, Pārtha, when,
obscured by darkness, it mistakes lawlessness for Law and
perceives all matters topsy-turvy.

That fortitude with which one sustains the operations
of mind, *prāṇas* and senses in unswerving yoga is of the
nature of *sattva*, Pārtha. The fortitude with which one
sustains Law, Profit, and Pleasure out of self-interest,
because one desires the rewards, Arjuna Pārtha, is of the
35 nature of *rajas*. While the fortitude with which a mindless
person does not rid himself of sleep, fear, grief, despair, and
inebriation is of the nature of *tamas*, Pārtha.

Hear from me now, bull of the Bharatas, about the
three kinds of happiness in which a person delights by
practising it assiduously and finds the end of his sorrows.
That is propounded to be happiness in *sattva* which at first
seems like poison but as it matures is like Elixir, the happiness which springs from the serenity of one's own spirit.
That happiness which springs from the contact of senses

with objects, and at first seems like Elixir but as it matures is like poison, is known as a product of *rajas*. The happiness which, at first and ever after, is the befuddlement of self which arises from sleep, sloth, and distraction is declared a product of *tamas*.

40 There is not a creature on earth, nor in heaven among the Gods, which is free from these three *guṇas* that spring from Prakṛti. The acts of brahmins, barons, commoners, and serfs, enemy-burner, divide themselves according to the *guṇas* that spring from nature. Tranquillity, self-control, austerity, purity, patience, honesty, insight, knowledge, and true faith are the brahmin's task, which derives from his nature. Gallantry, energy, fortitude, capability, unretreating steadfastness in war, liberality, and the exercise of power are the baron's task, which spring from his nature. Husbandry, cattle herding, and trade are the commoner's task, which derives from his nature; while the natural task of the serf is to serve.

45 Each man attains perfection by devoting himself to his own task: listen how the man who shoulders his task finds this perfection. He finds it by honouring, through the fulfillment of his own task, him who motivates the creatures to act, on whom all this is strung. One's own Law imperfectly observed is better than another's Law carried out with perfection. As long as one does the work set by nature, he does not incur blame. One should not abandon his natural task even if it is flawed, Kaunteya, for all undertakings are beset by flaws as fire is by smoke. He whose spirit is free from any personal interest in anything, who has conquered himself, who is rid of cravings, attains by his renunciation the ultimate perfection of freedom from *karman*.

50 Hear from me in brief, Kaunteya, how by reaching perfection one attains to *brahman*, which is the pinnacle of knowledge. Yoked with a pure spirit and subduing himself with fortitude, renouncing the sense objects of sound, etc,

and discarding love and hatred, seeking solitude, eating
lightly, restraining speech, body, and mind, intent upon the
yoga of contemplation, cultivating dispassion, ridding
himself of egotism, displays of strength, pride, lust, wrath,
and possessions, and being no longer acquisitive but
serene, he is able to become *brahman*. Having become
brahman, serene of spirit, he does not grieve, he does not
crave: equable to all creatures, he achieves the ultimate
55 *bhakti* of me. Through this *bhakti* he recognizes me for who
I am and understands how great I really am, and by virtue
of his true knowledge he enters me at once. Even though
performing all the acts, he has his shelter in me and by my
grace attains that supreme abode that is everlasting.

Relinquish all your acts to me with your mind, be
absorbed in me, embrace the yoga of the spirit, and always
have your mind on me. With your mind on me you will by
my grace overcome all hazards; but when you are too self-
centred to listen, you will perish. If you self-centredly
decide that you will not fight, your decision is meaningless
60 anyhow: your nature will command you. Fettered by your
own task, which springs from your nature, Kaunteya, you
will inevitably do what you in your folly do not want to do,
Arjuna. The lord of all creatures is inside their hearts and
with his wizardry he revolves all the creatures mounted on
his water wheel. Go to him for shelter with all your being,
Bhārata, and by his grace you shall reach the eternal abode
which is ultimate peace.

Reflect upon this knowledge I have propounded to you,
this mystery of mysteries, in its entirety, and then do as you
are pleased to do. Listen to one more final word of mine
that embodies the greatest mystery of all. I shall tell it for
65 your own good, for you are profoundly dear to me. Keep
your mind on me, honour me with your devotion and sacrifice, and you shall come to me. Abandon all the Laws and
instead seek shelter with me alone. Be unconcerned, I shall
set you free from all evils.

This is not to be revealed, ever, to one without austerities or devotion to me, nor to one who does not wish to listen or who disbelieves in me. But he who propounds to my devotees this ultimate mystery and thus shows me his perfect devotion shall beyond a doubt come to me. No one among humankind does me greater favour than he, nor shall anyone on earth be more dear to me than he.

70 He who commits to memory this our colloquy informed by Law, he will offer up to me a sacrifice of knowledge, so I hold. And he who, filled with belief and trust, listens to it, will be released and attain to the blessed worlds of those who have acted right.

Pārtha, have you listened to this with concentrated attention? Dhanaṃjaya, is your ignorant delusion now gone?

Arjuna said:
The delusion is gone, Acyuta, and by your grace I have recovered my wits. Here I stand with no more doubts. I shall do as you say.

Saṃjaya said:
Thus have I heard this Colloquy of Vāsudeva and the great-
75 spirited Pārtha, marvellous and enrapturing. By Vyāsa's grace I have heard this supreme mystery, this yoga, from that Master of Yoga Kṛṣṇa himself, who told it in person. Sire, whenever I reflect on this wondrous, holy Colloquy of Keśava and Arjuna, I rejoice anew. Whenever I recall that miraculous form of Hari, I am stunned to the core, sire, and rejoice anew. Wherever Kṛṣṇa the Master of Yoga and Pārtha the archer are, there, I hold, are fortune, victory, prosperity, and a steady course.

Notes to the translation

Text in square brackets is taken from Van Buitenen's original notes.

1

1 Dhṛtarāṣṭra: king-regent of the Kauravas, but not the 'acting' king, because of his blindness.

2 ie, *dharma* (*see* Introduction and 1: n. 34.)

3 Saṃjaya: [the old King Dhṛtarāṣṭra's personal bard, acts as his reporter on the progress of the war between the Pāṇḍavas, his nephews, and the Kauravas, his sons. After ten days Saṃjaya returns from the field with his first report.]

4 Duryodhana: eldest son of Dhṛtarāṣṭra and the 'acting' king of the Kauravas, but not of the whole 'disputed' kingdom of Kurukṣetra, over which the eldest of the Pāṇḍavas, Yudhiṣṭhira, remained the legitimate ruler.

5 Droṇa: the great guru of the Kauravas and, before the clan was split, the teacher of the younger (ie, the fourth) generation of both the Kauravas and the Pāṇḍavas. Though a brahmin, he was a great warrior and died on the battlefield, as Kṛṣṇa himself had determined (11:34).

6 Dhṛṣṭadyumna: [commander-in-chief of the Pāṇḍava forces.] He was the son of Drupada (*see* 1: n. 21) and a pupil of Droṇa.

7 Bhīma: second of the five Pāṇḍava brothers.

8 Saubhadra: [metronymic of Arjuna's son, Abhimanyu.] The name is taken from Subhadra, one of Arjuna's wives.

9 Draupadeyas: [the five sons of Draupadī by the five Pāṇḍavas.]

10 Bhīṣma: commander-in-chief of the Kauravas. He was Dhṛtarāṣṭra's paternal uncle and adoptive father. The only

surviving member of the second generation among the participants of the great battle.

11 Karṇa: premarital son of Kuntī by the Sun God and thus the elder half-brother of the first three Pāṇḍava brothers.

12 Kṛpa: [first teacher of the Pāṇḍavas] – before Droṇa.

13 Aśvatthāman: Droṇa's son.

14 ie, Bhīṣma.

15 Mādhava ('Honey-like'): an epithet of Kṛṣṇa.

16 ie, Arjuna, as one of the Pāṇḍavas.

17 Hṛṣīkeśa ('With bristling hair'): an epithet of Kṛṣṇa.

18 Dhanaṃjaya ('Purveyor of Wealth'): an epithet of Arjuna.

19 Wolf-Belly: an epithet of Bhīma (*see* 1: n. 7).

20 Śikhaṇḍin: Drupada's son and the Pāṇḍava's brother-in-law; the slayer of Bhīṣma (*see* 1: n. 10).

21 Drupada: king of South Panchala and the father-in-law of the five Pāṇḍava brothers who were married to his daughter Draupadī.

22 The sons of Dhṛtarāṣṭra.

23 Arjuna.

24 Acyuta ('Immovable', 'Unshakeable'): an epithet of Kṛṣṇa (as Viṣṇu).

25 Guḍākeśa ('Thick-haired' or 'bluish-black-haired'): an epithet of Arjuna.

26 Pārtha ('Son of Prithi'): an epithet of Arjuna (and of Yudhiṣṭhira and Bhīma). Prithi was another name of Kuntī, mother of the three elder Pāṇḍavas.

27 Keśava ('Hairy'): an epithet of Kṛṣṇa.

28 Govinda ('Cowherd'): an epithet of Kṛṣṇa.

29 Madhusūdana ('Slayer of the Demon Madhu'): an epithet of Kṛṣṇa.

30 Three Worlds: the world of gods, the world of men and the underworld.

31 Janārdana ('He who compels the men', or 'He who slays the (evil?) men'): an epithet of Kṛṣṇa (and Viṣṇu).

32 While objecting strongly to killing his cousins, the Kauravas, Arjuna maintains that he is *morally* right to blame them for being the real cause of the war. Being a simple, ordinary man, he could not help calling them assassins (his main 'objective' reason for doing so was Duryodhana's attempt to burn the Pāṇḍavas alive in a house fire, thwarted by their half-uncle Vidura).

33 Arjuna was saying that the split of the scions of the King Śamtanu which took place in the third generation (see the genealogical map) and their open struggle for power did not yet mean the destruction of the Law (*dharma*) of family. Only an outright and formally announced war (not sporadic incidents of individual hatred and enmity) destroys the eternal Law of Dharma and establishes lawlessness (*adharma*).

34 There were four classes (*varṇa*): *brahmins* (priests), *kṣatriyas* (warriors), *vaiṣyas* (farmers, merchants and artisans of 'pure' professions), and *sūdras* (servants and members of some 'impure' professions). Each *varṇa* was regulated by its specific class law (*varṇadharma*), which is not to be confused with non-class laws such as family laws, the law of kings, laws for each of the four stages of life (*aṣrama-dharma*), etc. Therefore, each man could be regarded as subject to and regulated by a whole 'cluster' of laws, each of which may have played a part in his choices and decisions.

35 'Class miscegenation' (*varṇaśamkāra*) is an extremely complex socio-cultural concept, at the core of which lies the idea that each class, taken separately in its 'purity', is better and purer than any mixture of classes. Thus, a child of a brahmin and a *sūdra* woman is lower in status (in terms of brahmanical purity) than either of its parents. Though, of course, this idea is a flagrant contradiction of the plot of the *Mahābhārata*, where the line of royal descent begins with the marriage of King Śamtanu to a fisherman's daughter, Satyāvati.

36 This is a direct reference to ancient Indian (broadly speaking, Vedic) religion and its veneration of ancestors (*pitars*). The dead ancestors depend almost entirely on the

sacrifices, oblations and prayers offered by their *male* progeny, without which they cannot survive in the world of ancestors and perish, disappearing into nowhere.

2

1 Noble (*ārya*): a general term denoting the members of the first three classes (*see* 1: n. 34), but applied particularly to the class of warriors.

2 'Nature', or more exactly, one's own nature (*svabhāva*), denotes the whole psychophysical complex of a person, the sum total of his innate tendencies, trends and attitudes. In this line the word is used as a synonym for 'character' or 'soul' (in an ordinary sense). As a general idea, it also means 'that which is individual and peculiar to a given person'.

3 It is interesting to note that whereas the reasons adduced by Arjuna at the end of the first chapter were *objective* (as related to Law, *Dharma*), here he simply does not want to fight – and hates the idea of it. This reluctance could be attributed to his individual nature (*svabhāva*). In other words, it would be wrong to say that Arjuna hates the war because it is against the Law (*dharma*); he simply regards it as lawless *and* hates it, at the same time.

4 'Creatures with bodies' or 'the embodied' (*dehin*): one of the most important notions of this book; synonymous with *Self* or Soul, ie, *ātman*.

5 'What did not already exist' (*asat*) means 'all that is not Self'. 'What does exist' (*sat*) is Self.

6 [ie, between being and nonbeing.] The boundary (or limit, extremity, *anta*) between what is Self and what is not Self, can be seen only by the wise (*paṇḍita*).

7 'Manifest and unmanifest' or 'clear and unclear' (*vyakta/avyakta*): the whole passage (25–29) is an expression of the idea that all things perceivable and thinkable have their origin in the imperceptible and unthinkable, continue as perceivable and thinkable, and then disappear into the unperceivable and unthinkable again. This idea is concretized here in the sense that only Self (as the embodied) is

unmanifest, as such, by definition. But between a man's unmanifest being, when his body is not yet born, and his body's disappearance in death, he is, as it were, manifest as that which abides in his body, since only the middle stage of all existences is manifested.

8 Your Law: ie, *your own* law (*svadharma*), which is your individual duty, *dharma*, and different from your professional, social or any other *dharma* (*see* 1: nn. 33 and 34). It is connected with and partly dependent on your own nature and character (*svabhāva*) and participates in your will and decisions. That is why the great Shankara writes in his *Commentary*: 'It was because his discrimination and practical knowledge were affected by grief and delusion that Arjuna did not want to fight, though he had voluntarily undertaken to fight his opponents as the *dharma of warriors*' (Ch 2, 11.0.a).

9 'A war that is lawful' here poses a bit of a problem: it is one thing for a warrior to fight a war out of his duty as a warrior (*kṣatriyadharma*) and/or out of personal loyalty to his sovereign (*svadharma*), which would make the war lawful *for him*; but the lawfulness of this particular war is quite another matter. Concerning the latter, Shankara writes: '[This] battle is [righteous] because it is for the sake of righteousness and people's security through the conquest of the world' (*op. cit.* Ch 2, 31, 1). This war would be deemed righteous, *dharmic* also, because, as will be seen in Chapter 11 of the *Gītā*, it had been predetermined, devised and staged by Lord Kṛṣṇa Himself.

10 'Spirit' here is a very conjectural rendering of *buddhi*, which has three main meanings:

1) [the psychophysical faculty of alertness and decisiveness];

2) the knowledge or understanding of a higher, or 'spiritual', order (as in Shankara, Ch 2, 39, 1);

3) the organ or faculty of such knowledge or understanding. While Shankara stresses the cognitive side of *buddhi*, Van Buitenen emphasizes its active, volitional function. Taken as an organ or faculty, *buddhi* can be regarded as a part, a level or an element of mind (*manas*), however superior it may be

to the rest of it. But there are other passages where, as another 'organ or faculty', it is opposed to mind. In the context of this passage, however, spirit (or *buddhi*) can be understood literally as 'that by means of which you (Arjuna) will understand what I (Kṛṣṇa) have told you'.

11 'Theory' (*sāṃkhya*) [has here the meaning of 'reflection'] – on 'things ultimate' (*paramārthavastu*) according to Shankara (*op. cit.*) Or it can be understood as general knowledge. In the *Bhagavad Gītā* it is that which requires a special application of spirit (*buddhi*) and is therefore opposed to 'practice' (*yoga*). At the same time, the term *sāṃkhya* is used here in the sense of 'a theory of universal dualism', anticipating the Sāṃkhya philosophy that was yet to appear (somewhere between the second and first century BC). From the beginning of Chapter 2, the term *sāṃkhya* also denotes the dualism of 'the Embodied (*ātman*)/(his) body' as well as the whole range of dualisms such as 'existent (*sat*)/non-existent (*asat*)', 'manifest/unmanifest', etc.

12 'Practice' (yoga) has three main meanings in the *Bhagavad Gītā*:

1)Practice as a conscious and purposeful *application* of any human faculty. In this passage, for example, the spirit (*buddhi*) is applied to the pursuit of 'cutting away the bondage of the act' (*see* below).

2) Practice as a specifically *yogic* activity which brings about a radical transformation of one or another mental or bodily function, habit, trend or attitude, or of the whole psychophysical organism. Understood in this sense, yoga comprises hundreds of *consciously* used methods, devices and instruments, from more general ones such as 'meditation', 'concentration of mind', 'disciplining (or taming) the mind' and 'working out the single-mindedness', to very particular and technical ones such as 'holding body, head and neck straight and immobile' (6:13).

3) Practice as any fact, event or circumstance in an individual's life which, not being consciously or intentionally produced by a person, induces him to become conscious of himself, and transforms his mind, speech and behaviour, or

makes them ready for a further yogic transformation in the sense of 1) and 2). That is why, according to a later tradition, each of the 18 chapters of the *Bhagavad Gītā* is prefixed with 'The yoga of'. Chapter 1, for example, is entitled 'The yoga of despondency of Arjuna', because it was the impending battle and Arjuna's despair which brought into realization the process of his instruction, effected by Kṛṣṇa, which led to his becoming a person with a yogically transformed consciousness.

13 'Bondage of the act' (*karmabandha*) refers to the idea (primarily purely ritualistic) that an act (*karman*: in compound nouns *karma*) binds a person who performs it in three ways. First, by motivations to perform it, such as desire, greed, hope, fear, etc. Second, by feelings and emotions accompanying its performance, such as hatred, love, anger, etc. Third, by the consequences of its performance. Only he who acts without any subjective motivation, emotion or expectation can cut away the bondage of action and become a *free agent*. This, according to the *Bhagavad Gītā*, is possible only for a person whose spirit is *yogically* applied to this task.

14 [In contradistinction to an act (*karman*) as defined by the Mīmāṃsakas, which can be voided by interruption or disruption, an act inspired by the single *buddhi* remains valid.] If a person is bound by his action, any omission, fault or interruption in its performance would mean a complete failure. While if he is free from the bondage of action, it does not, then, matter what happens to the performance or the performer – the action in this case is good by definition.

15 Law: [term borrowed from Mīmāṃsā, where *dharma* is tantamount to the (ritual) act.] Used here in the sense of 'the proper way of acting' (ie, as described above).

16 Kuru: the first king of the Lunar dynasty and common ancestor of both the Kauravas and Pāṇḍavas.

17 Disputations on the Veda: [arguments about how certain acts should be performed.] Sometimes these disputations

were about the minutest details in the performance of Vedic rituals or even about correctness of words and thoughts (intentions) preceding and accompanying these rituals. This, of course, contradicts directly the idea of freedom from the bondage of action (*see* 1: n. 14), on which Kṛṣṇa's critique of Vedic ritualism is based.

18 That there is nothing more (in the Vedas): 'They maintain that there is nothing in the Vedas other than rites which (if correctly and exactly performed) promise heaven, cattle, wealth and the like' (Shankara, Ch 2, 42).

19 Rebirth as the result of acts: The idea here is that not only is the form in which one is reborn (reincarnated) determined by one's good or bad actions (not only by rituals well or badly performed), but also whether one is reborn at all. Therefore, if a person does not act with a view to results and so is not bound by his actions (*see* 2:13), he will not be reborn.

20 Concentration (*samādhi*): a yogic method (*see* 2:12) which van Buitenen defines as [the emptying out from consciousness of all distracting perceptions and notions in order to concentrate on the ultimate object, an achievement impossible for the ritualists as long as they are enjoined to perform a variety of acts, many of which are *kāmya*, 'inspired by a specific desire', often enough a desire for pleasure (heaven, son, rain, etc) and dominion (overlordship, etc)].

21 The three *guṇas* are the three main *dynamic tendencies* which constitute the phenomenal world or *nature* (*prakṛti*): *rajas* – passion, activity, creativeness, centrifugal movement, its symbolic colour red; *tamas* – sloth, stupor, passivity, dissolution, centripetal movement, its symbolic colour black; *sattva* – dispassion, equanimity, balance, meditativeness, circular movement, its symbolic colour white. Saying that 'the domain of the Vedas is the world of the three *guṇas*' means that the aim and motivation of the Vedic rituals are confined to the material, natural world of human desires and their fulfilment.

22 Beyond the pairs of opposites (*nirdvaṃdva*): transcending such vulgar oppositions of ordinary life as good/bad,

friendly/hostile, hot/cold, correct/incorrect, right/wrong, etc. Only those who have already understood that which *is* beyond all oppositions, ie, the embodied, *ātman*, can, in their application of this understanding, train themselves to think, speak and act without using those normal human oppositions.

23 Entitlement (*adhikāra*): the sum total of requirements which entitle a person to perform a specific action (usually a Vedic ritual). Entitlement is, normally, a rule or injunction in the form of a conditional clause, wherein the second proposition constitutes an entitlement proper. So, according to the Mīmāṃsā school of Indian philosophy, 'if a Vedic injunction declares that he who desires heaven should perform a ritual called Glorifying the Fire', [it is specifically his desire to obtain heaven that *entitles* him to perform this ritual] – and receive its fruit (ie, obtain heaven). In the *Bhagavad Gītā*, however, Kṛṣṇa, contrary to Mīmāṃsā, states that 'entitlement is only to the ritual, not . . . to its fruits', and that the ritual ought to be performed without any desire for its fruits. In both cases, entitlement is always derived from a higher authority: a sacred text, or a school of its traditional commentators, or a god, etc.

24 Equableness (*samatva*, lit. 'sameness'): one of the methods of yogic practice (*see* 2: n. 12.2), and one of the applications (also yoga, *see* 2: n. 12.1) of the spirit of a practitioner to the pursuance of complete single-mindedness.

25 Good and evil *karman*: any action intended, thought or desired (as the ritual in 2: n. 23) for the sake of its good or bad consequences (results, fruits). And one's good or bad actions determine not only whether one has a good or bad rebirth, but whether one is reborn at all (*see* 2: nn. 13 and 19).

26 Capacity to act: capacity to act without any desire for results, which in itself is regarded as a means of making an action successful.

27 Bondage of rebirth: connected with and following from the bondage of action. (*see* 2: nn. 13, 19 and 25).

28 'The revealed' (*śruti*, lit. 'the heard') has two meanings:

1) The Vedas and the knowledge of the sacred texts;

2) any other knowledge and all that was learnt (heard) by a person before he embarked on the path of yoga offered by Kṛṣṇa.

29 'Insight' (*prajñā*) denotes here a kind of superknowledge accessible only to those whose spirit is applied to yoga.

30 Withdraws: [though he may see, he will not look; he may hear but not listen, etc.]

31 He does not eat: in the sense that he does not enjoy his food. 'Food' here is a metaphor for all objects of enjoyment, all things enjoyable by the organs of sense. [Figuratively, he who does not feed on, thrive on, external objects.]

32 Taste (*rasa*): an abstract quality of things enjoyable – abstract in the sense that even when one does not actually (or physically) enjoy an object, that quality exists in one's mind as the *subtlest perception*. So the gods enjoy the sacrificial food by 'eating its smoke' during a sacrifice.

33 Last hour (*antakāla*): an absolutely decisive factor in one's post-mortal existence, for it provides even a simple ordinary person with a yogic capacity for supernatural concentration of thought and memory.

34 *Nirvāṇa*: the complete forsaking of all worldly conditions and bonds and 'being one with the *Brahman*' (*brahmanirvāṇa*). (Note that at that time this term was used in a much broader context than that of Buddhism.)

3

1 Even the yoga (discipline) itself is action.

2 Three forces: [the three *guṇas.*] (*see* 2: n. 21.)

3 Faculties of action: tongue, hands, feet, anus and genitals.

4 Disinterested (*asakta*): 'having no (personal) interest in an action, nor desiring its fruit' – as opposed to 'interested' (or 'involved'). The general idea conveyed is that only disinterested actions, of whatever kind, are pure and constitute the sacrifice to Kṛṣṇa.

5 For purposes of sacrifice: selfless sacrifice, performed for the sake of sacrifice itself.

6 Prajāpati: a Vedic god, the creator of all creatures and establisher of the Vedic sacrifices. Later he became partly identified with the god Brahmā.

7 *Brahman* of the Veda: [ie, its sacred contents.] According to Shankara (Ch 3, 1S.1): '[This] ritual action is born of *Brahman* and revealed by the Veda. *Brahman is* the Veda. This *Brahman* is born of the Imperishable *Brahman*, the Supreme Self (*paramātman*), the Imperishable Person (*puruṣa*).'

8 *OṂ*: [the *akṣara*, to which the entire Veda can be meaningfully reduced.] *Akṣara* (the indestructible) is also the central sound-symbol (*mantra*) in practically all ancient Indian religions. The syllable itself (as a pure sound without any signification) is regarded as the *ultimate essence* of all that is sacred and eternal.

9 The Wheel (*cakra*): symbol of universal dynamism, of the cosmic power of change and transformation. It is particularly significant in Buddhism.

10 Janaka: the king of Videha (in northeast India) and one of the wisest men in ancient India – [imbued with the true spirit of Veda and sacrifice].

11 Vārṣṇeya: a man of the Vrishni clan, to which Kṛṣṇa belonged by his human birth.

12 *See* 2: n. 21.

13 Bharata: the name of the dynasty and the tribe to which both the Pāṇḍavas and Kauravas belonged.

14 'He' here is Self, *ātman*.

4

1 Vivasvat: the Sun god in the Vedas.

2 Manu: Vivasvat's son, the first man and the ancestor of all mankind.

3 Ikṣvāku: Manu's great-grandson and the founder of the Solar dynasty.

4 Wizardry (*māyā*): the divine creative energy of Kṛṣṇa. The term *māyā*, when used in the sense of the cosmic or universal illusion, means that those who are devoid of the higher knowledge cannot see that all things are created by Kṛṣṇa's *māyā*, and instead regard them as really existent.

5 The meaning of the whole sentence is that a pure action (without motivation and desire) has no *karman* (no good or bad consequences, including *karmic* consequences relating to future rebirths), while non-action, when motivated and desired, is *karman*.

6 'Self' here is not Self (*ātman*), but rather 'your whole self', ie, including your body and your senses and emotions.

7 One who acts sacrifically: a person to whom all actions are like a ritual performed for ritual's sake only.

8 In verses 24–25, *brahman* is used to denote all stages and constituents of the sacrificial action, including its invisible transcendental basis and essence.

9 Offer the senses: [practise withdrawal of sensory activity] – by means of yogic control.

10 [Here *prāṇa* and *apāna* clearly have the sense of inhalation and exhalation.] (For more details on yogic breathing *see* 15: n. 2.)

11 Mouth of Brahman: [the sacrificial fire, both figurative and literal.]

5

1 Nine-gated fortress: [the body, its 'gates' being the orifices.]

2 Nature (*svabhāva*): its use here is rather ambiguous, for though on the one hand it is nature in general (*prakṛti*, *see* 2: n. 21) that initiates acts, on the other it can also be one's own (ie, individual) nature.

3 To return again: to be reborn.

4 Eater of dog: a notion of utmost degradation – dog meat has been absolutely taboo from time immemorial. (It is mentioned in the Rig Veda, where the god Indra, when starving, ate dog's intestines.)

6

1 [ie, the Buddhists and other unorthodox who reject the Vedic ritual.]

2 Beyond *nirvāṇa*: that which cannot be described or thought of as any state of religious enlightenment, however high, or ultimate aim of religious (or yogic) experience – an unfathomable absolute.

3 Either way: both practically, in his pursuit of ordinary activity, and yogically, in his pursuit of the ultimate goal.

4 Merit (*puṇya*): that which karmically (ie, in other rebirths) gains one a higher (divine) status and superhuman bliss. However, to achieve the highest status, one would have to be reborn human. This last condition is common to almost all religio-philosophical teachings of ancient India.

7

1 Ether: [*ākāśa*, which is held to be the medium of sound.]

2 Vāsudeva: the main (patronymic) name of Kṛṣṇa in his 'human' manifestation.

3 Illusion of my Yoga: the illusion (*māyā*, *see* 4: n. 4) produced by Kṛṣṇa's divine yoga.

4 When bad karmic consequences of previous actions have been exhausted.

8

1 The self of a living being is called 'nature' in the sense of another or higher nature of Kṛṣṇa (*see* 8: 4–6).

2 'Spirit' (*puruṣa*) here is a concretization of 'an individual, living (or animate) being (*bhūta*)' in the sense of 'this or that creature having its nature', etc.

3 'Sacrificial' here in this body: [the one to whom all sacrifices are directed] – *brahman*, core and basis of each and every ritual.

4 [ie, in a new life one derives new being from that of which one thinks at the hour of death.]

5 'World of Brahmā' has two meanings. In the first, it is the whole sphere of creation, comprising all concrete worlds of men, gods, etc, created by the god Brahmā. Its second meaning refers to the highest abode of divine beings, where their lifespan is longer than in any other world. Here we deal with the second meaning.

6 Return eternally: again and again they are reborn in the places, times and states determined by their *karma*. This also may mean that they return to the human state.

7 Returns: is born again.

9

1 Do not exist in me: though all creatures exist in Kṛṣṇa in the sense of his higher nature (*see* 7: 4–6 and 7: n. 1), they do not exist in him in the sense of his highest and all-transcending unmanifest being.

2 Supernal yoga: Kṛṣṇa's highest superdivine energy which creates the universal *māyā*.

3 By the force of my nature: by the energy issued from *His own* nature, which is the primary and eternal source of all cosmic changes and processes and cannot be other than that which it is, for He Himself is unchangeable. [This inherent creative and destructive pulsation of God is automatic.]

4 Asuras: the sky gods in the Vedic (and possibly, pre-Vedic) religion. Later they became anti-gods, like the Titans in ancient Greek mythology.

5 Rākṣasas: flesh-eating demons. The group of evil spirits most hostile to man.

6 'The herb' here probably refers to the main sacrificial plant, soma, not yet identified with any known plant. In a special preparation ritual the soma was pressed, fermented and strained and then offered to the gods as the elixir of immortality.

7 Formula: mantra (*see* 3: n. 8).

8 Butter: sacrificial melted butter burnt on the sacrificial fire.

9 Strainer: the strainer used in the preparation of soma (*see* n. 6 above).

10 *Ṛc (rig)*, *sāman* and *yajus* refer to the three Vedas: the Rig Veda (the Veda of hymns – rig is one of the four classes of mantra, with a fixed metre and accentuation); the Sama Veda (*sāman* is the melody of the Vedic verses); and the Yajus Veda (*yajus* is a sacrificial formula recited during the Vedic ritual).

11 Domain of Indra: Indra is the chief god in the Vedic pantheon, the king of gods, the leader and protector of warriors, and the god of the atmosphere (not of heaven proper), especially of the elemental forces of storm, rain, thunder and lightning. He is identified with the idea of military force, manly energy and kingly power. His domain or paradise is the place where gods and god-like great men abide.

12 Ghouls (*bhūtas*) [the ghosts of those deceased whose remains have not properly been disposed of by ceremonial cremation.]

13 *Vaiśyas*, nay *sūdras*: *see* 1: n. 34.

10

1 The four Manus: the first four mortal (though supernatural) men, of whom Manu (*see* 4: n. 2) was the first.

2 'Ubiquity' (*vibhūti*) denotes divine transformations produced by Kṛṣṇa's *māyā*, including his appearances in various forms and aspects and his descents (*avatāras*) to earth. The most striking feature of ubiquity is that Kṛṣṇa, while appearing in one form (as Arjuna's charioteer, say) can appear in another form at that same place, or somewhere else, and at the same time remain His unfathomable, unchanging Self and Person.

3 Filled with being: filled with the (knowledge of) Kṛṣṇa's reality – a very ambiguous metaphor.

4 My stories: the stories of Kṛṣṇa's miraculous births (eg, as Vāsudeva), spectres and other ubiquities (*see* n. 2 above).

5 Nārada: [a seer and frequent visitor from the gods] – to whom several Vedic hymns are ascribed.

6 Asita Devala and Vyāsa: the former is a great ascetic from the family of Kāṣyapa; the second, also a great ascetic, was the real father of both Pāṇḍu and Dhṛtarāṣṭra.

7 Dānavas: a group of demons in the Vedic mythology.

8 Ādityas: the twelve sons of Aditi, the female manifestation of the solar element of creation. The most prominent among them were the gods Indra, Sūrya (sun), and Viṣṇu.

9 Maruts: the storm gods and sons of the god Rudra (wherefrom their other name, Rudras). Marīchi, one of the ten mind-born sons of the god Brahmā, figures here as one of the Maruts.

10 Vāsava: an epithet of the god Indra (lit. 'he to whom the gods of Vasu class belong').

11 'Consciousness' (*cetanā*) is regarded here as a higher order of being: some beings have only the five (or fewer) sensory organs, some have the five senses plus mind, but only humans and gods have consciousness.

12 Rudras: *see* n. 9 above.

13 Śaṃkara: an epithet of Shiva (lit. 'appeasing' or 'healing').

14 Yakṣas: supernatural beings who are guardians of the treasures of the God of Riches (Kubera).

15 Vasus: an order of deities (*see* n. 10 above).

16 Meru: the mythical mountain in the centre of the world, made of gold and jewels.

17 Bṛhaspati: the chief priest of gods, the family priest and the preceptor of Indra. Astrologically he is identified with the planet Jupiter.

18 Skanda: [the army commander of the gods] – and son of Rudra (or Shiva).

19 Bhṛgu: a great Vedic seer.

20 One syllable: the mantra *OṂ* (*see* 3: n. 8).

21 Aśvattha: the sacred fig tree possessing some supernatural qualities. It is also the symbol of the universal cosmic arrangement.

22 Gandharvas (lit. 'smell-eaters'): a class of Vedic semi-gods. They are celestial musicians and singers, capable of flying in the air. Citraratha is their king.

23 Siddhas: a special class of ascetics who possess the supernatural power (*siddhi*). Kapila is a most powerful siddha born from the seminal essence of Viṣṇu (or Kṛṣṇa).

24 Elixir: of immortality (*amṛta*).

25 Airāvata: the elephant of Indra.

26 The Cow of Plenty: the mythical cow capable of fulfilling all human desires (of material character).

27 Kandarpa: [the god of love] – another name of Kāma.

28 Vāsuki: a king of the class of magical snakes (*nāgas*) associated mythologically with the element of water (they are rain givers).

29 Ananta ('Infinite'): the Divine Serpent on which Viṣṇu reposes.

30 Varuṇa: one of the most important gods of the Vedic pantheon; guardian of Cosmic Order and mythologically associated with the element of water.

31 Aryaman: the god of the ancestors; a solar deity and the god of hospitality.

32 Yama: the god of death in the Vedic and Hindu pantheons, a brother of Manu (*see* 4: n. 2).

33 Daityas: an order of anti-gods born from the demoness Diti and great seer Kāṣhyapa. Prahlāda was the greatest Daitya, and mighty rival of the god Indra.

34 Kāla ('time'): Time personified.

35 'Things that count', according to Van Buitenen, are things that are the basis for counting ['counting off']. His other conjecture here is that Time is the all-cosmic factor that impels all things towards their end and destruction (*see* 11: 25–30).

36 Garuḍa: the king of birds and the divine vehicle of Viṣṇu.

37 Rāma (alias Paraśu-Rāma, 'Rāma with Axe'): the sixth *avatāra* ('descent') of the god Viṣṇu and an ally of the Kauravas.

38 The '*a*': the first sound in the Sanskrit alphabet, and the shortest magical syllable (mantra, *see* 3: n. 8).

39 *Dvaṃdva*: the double compound in Sanskrit grammar, as in 'King Warrior', 'Youth Nobleman', etc.

40 Sāmans: *see* 9: n. 10.

41 Gāyatrī: the famous Vedic hymn to the Sun and the metric formula (mantra) of this hymn.

42 Mārgāśīrṣa: the ninth month of the Indian lunar calendar (November–December).

43 Vāsudeva: *see* 7: n. 2.

44 I am . . . Arjuna: this identification of Kṛṣṇa with his friend and interlocutor, Arjuna, can be read in various ways. The first conjecture is that Kṛṣṇa identifies himself with 'the best in (or among) everything', and with Arjuna as the best among Pāṇḍavas. The second is that he loves his friend Arjuna so much that he is 'one with him'. The third is that Kṛṣṇa means that he is Arjuna's self (*ātman*).

45 Vyāsa: *see* 10: n. 6.

46 Kavi Uśanas: the great seer and the priest and preceptor of the Asuras (*see* 9: n. 4). He is the son of Bhṛgu (*see* 10: n. 19) and is associated with the planet Venus.

11

1 Aśvins ('horsemen'): twin sons of the Divine Mare and the Sun God, the great healers and gods of morning and evening twilight in the Vedic pantheon. They were the real fathers of Arjuna's younger brothers, Nakula and Sahadeva.

2 Hari ('green', 'tawny', 'reddish-brown', 'yellowish'): an epithet of Kṛṣṇa and Viṣṇu.

3 *See above* 8: 21.

4 Sādhyas: a group of deities of ascetic character.

5 All-Gods: the group of ten gods supposed to be sons of Brahmā.

6 *Sūta*: charioteer, usually fulfilling also the function of a bard. Bhāradvāja, the father of Droṇa, was a *sūta* in the latter sense.

7 Left-handed Archer: an epithet of Arjuna, denoting his rare ability to shoot arrows with his left hand.

8 Jayadratha: the King of Sindhu and Dhṛtarāṣṭra's son-in-law.

9 Yādava ('Descendant of Yadu'): an epithet of Krishna, who in his human aspect was born into a family whose remotest ancestor was King Yadu.

10 *Tapas* (lit. 'heat'): a form of extreme asceticism, and a special supernatural power (or energy) produced by it.

11 *Bhakti*: here one of the central notions of the religion of the *Bhagavad Gītā*, meaning one's *absolute devotion* to Kṛṣṇa the Lord, one's complete mutual absorption with Him.

12

1 [ie, those who pursue the knowledge and attainment of the *ātman* alone.]

2 'Standing on the peak' can have [two possible explanations: 1) 'Standing at the top of the crown of the head' (which is one of the well-known yogic postures; 2) 'Standing on the top of a mountain', and thus taking a disinterested view of things . . .].

13

1 *Brahmasūtras* can have here two meanings:

1) [Technically a corpus of *sūtras* about *brahman*, ascribed to Bādarāyana] (c. first century AD);

2) Texts about *brahman* in general.

2 The Elements (or Primary Elements): earth, water, fire, air and ether (or space).

3 *Ahaṃkāra* (lit. 'I-factor', or 'I-ness', 'Ego-ness'): a special mental organ of one's awareness (and feeling) of oneself as 'I' ('me', 'mine', etc).

4 The ten Faculties: the five faculties of sensory perception and the five faculties of action (*see* 3: n. 3).

5 The five Realms: the five spheres of objects of the five organs of the senses.

6 Evolutes: all that which evolves from the primary, unmanifest nature (*prakṛti*).

7 *Puruṣa*: used here in the sense it has in the ancient Indian philosophical system of Sāṃkhya, it denotes the Conscious Principle of the Universe. Conscious and in itself unchanging, it is thus opposed to Nature (*prakṛti*), which is ever evolving.

8 Introspection (*dhyāna*): a technical term denoting a special yogic practice.

14

1 Are not reborn: ie, when a new world is created by the god Brahmā, they (more exactly their selves, *ātmans*) are not reincarnated but remain in a pure, disembodied state.

2 'Nor do they suffer at the time of dissolution' means that they do not disappear as *persons*, but continue to exist with their unimpaired memory and full awareness of themselves.

3 'Pure Worlds' may have two meanings:

1) pure socio-cultural conditions of birth (eg, being born into a brahmanic family)

2) celestial worlds, like the Vaikuṇṭha, the paradise of Viṣṇu.

15

1 Aśvattha tree: *see* 10: n. 21.

2 *Prāṇa* and *apāna*: two main notions of psychophysical activity. As a general term, *prāṇa* is 'life-force', 'principle of animatedness', and 'breathing' in general. In a more specific and technical sense it denotes the flows of air in the human organism. *Apāna* is 'breathing out', 'respiration', 'the life-wind' that goes downward and out of the anus. Both are most important in the process of digestion.

3 The four kinds of food: hot, sweet, sour and pungent.

4 Vedānta here does not refer specifically to the Vedānta school of ancient Indian philosophy; rather, it means all speculative and theoretical interpretations of Vedic ritualism, symbolism and ideas.

17

1 *OṂ tat sat* is a threefold mantra (*see* 3: n. 8). Literally, *sat* means 'that which is real' (*brahman*), and *tat* means 'that'.

18

1 Keśin: a malevolent Rākṣasa (*see* 9: n. 5) killed by Kṛṣṇa.

2 Divine fate (*daiva*): a very complex concept meaning specifically the interference of divine forces and supernatural factors in one's life. Sometimes it determines the character of one's death.

Further Reading

Alston, A J, *Samkara Source Book*, Shanti Sadan, London
Edgerton, F, *The Bhagavad Gītā*, Harvard University Press, 1944
Lamotte, Etienne, *Notes sur le Gītā*, Geuthner, Paris, 1929
Radhakrishnan, S, *The Bhagavad Gītā*, Allen and Unwin, London, 1948
Zaehner, R C, *The Bhagavad-gītā*, Oxford University Press, 1969